CONCILIUM

Religion in the Eighties

CONCILIUM

Editorial Directors

General Secretariat: Prins Bernhardstraat 2, 6521 AB Nijmegen, The Netherlands

Concilium 192 (4/1987): Dogma

CONCILIUM

List of Members

Advisory Committee: Dogma

ORTHODOXY
AND
HETERODOXY

Edited by
Johann-Baptist Metz
and
Edward Schillebeeckx

English Language Editor
Marcus Lefébure

T. & T. CLARK LTD
Edinburgh

August 1987
T. & T. Clark Ltd, 59 George Street, Edinburgh EH2 2LQ
ISBN: 0 567 30072 2

ISSN: 0010-5236

Typeset by C. R. Barber & Partners (Highlands) Ltd, Fort William
Printed by Page Brothers (Norwich) Ltd

Concilium: Published February, April, June, August, October, December.
Subscriptions 1987: UK: £24.95 (including postage and packing); USA: US$45.00 (including air mail postage and packing); Canada: Canadian$55.00 (including air mail postage and packing); other countries: £24.95 (including postage and packing).

CONTENTS

Part III
Practical Aspects

CONCILIUM 192 Special Column

Leonardo Boff

The Poor Judge: The Magisterium and Liberation Theologians

Before there was a theology of liberation, there was liberating pastoral work: prophetic bishops, Christians taking part in processes of social change, critical analysis of underdevelopment as the reverse side of the coin of development, identification of the mechanisms that generate poverty, discovery of the transforming and evangelising potential of the poor, the base Christian communities. ... These make up a social and ecclesial reality, on which liberation theology reflects. Its greatest achievement is to have placed the poor—their cause, their struggles and their lives as well as their Christological centrality to the Gospel and the sacraments—in the position of central challenge to Christian thought and practice. For liberation theologians, the poor are not just one subject among others on their agenda, but the privileged locus theologicus *for better understanding the Christian message as good news, God as the one who intervenes in history in favour of the oppressed, Jesus Christ as redeemer and liberator of all, beginning with the poor; the mission of the Church as bearer and enabler of integral liberation, and other associated themes.*

The commitment of the Churches to the poor against their poverty and the theology that legitimises and sheds light on this action (liberation theology) have lent universal credibility to the Christian faith, confirmed by so many Christians who have given their lives in defence of the oppressed. A major sign of our times is the movement of the poor to take stock of the oppressions they suffer, to organise themselves and embark on their own liberation. The churches are taking part in this struggle for reasons intrinsic to their very faith; it is not the churches that will liberate the poor: the organised poor liberate themselves, but they find valuable allies in major sections of the churches. How have the doctrinal authorities in Rome reacted to this current of theological development? And how were the two Instructions from the Congregation for the Doctrine of the Faith, Libertatis Nuntius of 1984 and Libertatis Conscientia of 1986 received? To consider Rome's reaction to liberation theology first:

Rome receives theological thinking from the 'periphery' in a manner conditioned by its understanding of itself as 'the centre'. It does not put itself in the place of the poor; it sees them with the eyes of the rich. This makes it adopt a pastoral strategy of assistance: the Church acts for the poor, never with the poor or starting from the viewpoint of the poor themselves. In the Instructions, genuine liberation has to be mediated through the Church. This fails to give theologal value to the struggles of the oppressed outside the Christian sphere.

They also show a tendency to spiritualise liberation, which is seen principally as liberation from sin, without specifying what sin is involved: the social sin of hunger, exploitation and premature death.

There is still an inveterate mistrust of everything to do with Marxism, and of the people as conscious and active agents of their own liberation. Marxism is seen as threatening the existence of the Church, the conscious people as threatening its power.

All this is strong on doctrine, but weak on prophecy and pastoral vision. Rome 'does' its liberation theology without any input from those bishops whose pastoral outlook gives primacy to the people and who first identified the need and set the agenda for liberation. There is little self-criticism and a great deal of institutional arrogance.

How were these documents received in Latin America? The first, which dealt mainly with the relationship between Marxism and liberation theology, was more criticised than welcomed, because of its caricature of liberation theologians. The second document was better received. Despite its internal limitations, it made a favourable impression on public opinion and in Christian circles: Rome supports liberation theology! The reasons given by the local churches and their theologians were not always the same as those contained in the two Instructions. For ordinary Christians struggling in their communities, theological niceties matter little, but it was important for them to feel they were being supported, that reinforcements were being brought to the front line, so to speak.

Basically, the Instructions accepted the legitimacy of a theology of liberation within a theology of consequences (Konsequenstheologie);

liberation is a fruit of redemption (soteriological liberation) which impinges on social reality (ethico-social liberation). The evangelical and ecclesial character of the preferential option for the poor was also accepted. Appreciation was also expressed for the base communities, popular Catholicism, and 'the Church of the poor' or 'the people's Church' (acceptably understood) as entities demonstrating the process of liberation within the Church itself.

Finally, the Instructions recognised that liberation theology has thrown down a challenge that has to be taken up by all theologians, who must seek to include the liberation dimension in all their works: 'It is not possible to ignore, for a single moment, the situations of dramatic poverty from which the challenge issued to theologians springs' (LN, IV, 1). In John Paul II's letter to the bishops of Brazil, of 9 April 1986, he recognised that liberation theology is 'not just opportune but useful and necessary'. These are at least minimal supports with which liberation theologians can carry on their work, in the conviction that both they and the magisterium *are being judged by the poor: they will tell us if we are effectively helping their liberation and how far we are, with them, helping forward the coming of the Kingdom.*

Translated by Paul Burns

Note that this Special Column, like others in this series, is written under the sole responsibility of the author.

ORTHODOXY AND HETERODOXY

Editorial

THERE ARE two main reasons making for the urgency of the topic of orthodoxy in the context of the Dogma section of *Concilium*.

The first reason is tied to the intellectual and spiritual situation of the time we live in: a time that is characterised by many people—and especially in Europe and America—as '*post-modern*'. It is a situation in which there is a release from the demand for truth and universality made by so-called modernity; in which multiplicity has taken logical and practical priority over unity; in which monotheism has fallen foul of the suspicion of totalisation and in which mythical polytheism has correspondingly won new disciples; a situation in which everything is possible and allowed but in which nothing is binding. In such a situation all talk and requirement of 'orthodoxy' must appear to be outworn. For it is only where universalist principles for the interpretation and handling of the world are still maintained, where hunger and thirst for truth have not yet been exhausted that the talk and struggle for 'orthodoxy' has any purchase. In this sense the theme of 'orthodoxy-heterodoxy' may originate from within theology but it can serve to challenge the *Zeitgeist*: it can, at least in an indirect fashion, serve to decipher the signature of our present age and to test the conventional wisdom of suspecting all talk of orthodoxy of being totalitarian.

It goes without saying that a second reason for choosing this theme was central to our preoccupation. In the last issue of this section of Dogma (1985) we discussed the question of the extent to which ordinary believers have teaching authority in the church as well as the official teaching office. We gave this question a consistently affirmative answer, in no small measure based as it was on Newman's concept of the authority of the faithful in matters of belief and stamped as it also was by an understanding of the Church rooted in the most recent council. This already touched upon the question of the appropriate understanding and the divers bearers of a Church orthodoxy that should not be a matter just of an élite or of experts. As already indicated, it was this second reason that proved decisive in the choice of theme, and this is also why it has shaped the composition of this issue. This number is divided into three parts.

The *first part* focuses on *exegetical and historical aspects*, albeit with systematic overtones. We hardly need to say that none of these three parts pretends to an exhaustive treatment of the topic but that it seeks to expose various facets of the problem and to open up insights from many disciplines into the discussion of the theme that is going on today. The first two articles deal with the different ways in which the question of orthodoxy presents itself in the Old Testament and in the New Testament traditions and also in post-Christian Judaism and in post-biblical Christianity. In his contribution 'Orthodoxy and Orthopraxis in the Old Testament' *E. Zenger* expounds a 'kairologico-dialogical orthodoxy' in the Old Testament traditions that is also very relevant to the Christian traditions, and *A. Paul* for his part in a 'systematic comparison' between (post-Christian) Judaism and (post-biblical) Christianity comes to the conclusion that the markedly centrifugal Christian system forces the question of orthodoxy out into the open whereas the more centripetal system of Judaism (not least in view of its 'open' messianism) puts the need, even the capacity for orthodoxy into question. *J. McCue* returns to glean the work of W. Bauer that has in the meantime become classical, *Rechtgläubigkeit und Ketzerei im ältesten Christentum*, and stresses that this work was not really about the doctrinal content of early Christianity but about the question of the relationship between faith, theological reflection and history, about a question, therefore, that does nevertheless belong to the understanding of the development of the notion of orthodoxy.

The *second part* of our issue is concerned with *selected systematic aspects* of the topic of orthodoxy-heterodoxy. Thus *A. Houtepen* explores a question that, at least since the last council, is closely bound up with our theme: the question of the meaning of the principle of the 'hierarchy of truths'. The author expounds the relevant statements of the council, discusses the ecumenical meaning of the formula, 'hierarchy of truths', and concludes by emphasising that the concept of orthodoxy itself connotes a process, a sort of movement of search. In his investigation of the concept of truth in African theology *A. Ngindu Mushete* discusses a particular example of the relationship between orthodoxy or unity of dogmatic teaching and cultural context, a question that is destined to become ever more urgent for the Church as it becomes a culturally polycentric world Church. *J. Moingt* detects in the famous Pauline dictim 'Oportet et haereses esse' (1 Cor. 11:19) a concept of heresy that does not attach a narrowing and impoverishing sense to the familiar opposition between orthodoxy and heterodoxy for the community of believers but that can rather have a creative function in the ecumenical struggle for the *Una Sancta*. In his article, 'Orthodoxy in the Dialectic of Theory and Practice', *T. Peters* concentrates on the fundamental theologico-epistemological question that is included in our theme: In view of the present discussion about the practical basis of Church teaching, the significance and problem of which is usually obscured rather than illuminated by the use of the word 'orthopraxis', Peters speaks about the doctrinal and, in a larger sense, political conditions that must be constantly and simultaneously taken into account in such a way that the understanding of orthodoxy is neither 'purely pragmatic' nor 'purely objective'. The last two articles of the second part deal with the important problem of the relationship between orthodoxy and the institution or institutionalising of the knowing of truth. This is the relevance of the attentiveness to Church institutions for the maintenance of orthodoxy and unity of belief that *G. Alberigo*, with all his characteristic sensitivity to Church history, bids us have. And *I. Fetscher* for his part concerns himself with two examples of the relationship between orthodoxy and heterodoxy outside the Church and religion (Marxist theory and Leninist party orthodoxy; secular attitudes towards orthodoxy in psycho-analytical infighting).

The *third part* of this issue deals finally with certain *practical and pastoral aspects* of the theme, though they do of course feed back into the theological and systematic understanding of orthodoxy and heterodoxy. *H. Vorgrimler* deals—and in a way that nobody else has done with such finesse and thoroughness—with the probabilities and problems involved in the now public project to draw up a *world catechism* meant to ensure the unity of belief in a culturally polycentric and socially divided world Church. The articles by *A. Moreira* and *D. Sölle* tackle the question of the extent to which a given social and political line of conduct can split the community of faith and thereby touch on the notion of orthodoxy. Moreira deals with the Brazilian context and considers the theological assessment of the excommunication of politicians and owners of great estates on the part of the bishops of the country, while Sölle interprets apartheid in South Africa as a challenge that raises the question of truth and thereby summons Christians to become a confessing Church. And, to conclude, *F. Biot* contests the understanding of orthodoxy that emerges from cardinal Ratzinger's book *Conversation on the Faith*.

We hope that this issue of our review will make some—naturally not entirely uncontroverted—contribution to ecclesial and Christian understanding in the truth and to the clarification of the requirement of truth in an age that under the influence of modern slogans all too easily distances itself from the notion 'that we thinkers of today, we godless and anti-metaphysical people, still take our fire from a brand that lit a thousand year old faith, that Christian faith that was also the faith of Plato, that God is truth, that truth is divine' (F. Nietzsche).

Johann-Baptist Metz
Edward Schillebeeckx

Translated by John Maxwell

PART I

Exegetical and Historical Aspects

Erich Zenger

Orthodoxy and Orthopraxis in the Old Testament

1. THE NECESSITY OF THEOLOGICAL CONTROVERSY

'THERE IS no such thing as an Old Testament theology', wrote Emil Brunner, the systematic theologian.[1] And he was not without arguments on his side. The writings and books gathered together into the library we know as the Old Testament are so varied in teaching and style that it really is *impossible to turn them into a global doctrinal system*. So the Epistle to the Hebrews was not so wide of the mark in maintaining (1:1) that 'God spoke of old to our fathers in many and various ways'. Even if we define theology in the less narrow and systematic sense, it is still true to say that 'the Old Testament contains, not merely one theology but a whole number; and these diverge widely from each other'.[2] If this is so, will it not be permissible for us to conclude that the Old Testament is the inspired protest against every 'theology' which is on the look out (or has to be, to survive) for the criteria of *a single* orthodoxy in saying what it thinks it has to say, in the light of its own inward passion?

On the other hand, it is unmistakably plain that there was a *conflict about the truth in Old Testament Israel*—a conflict not infrequently fought with the gloves off, at least by the people who represented the State and/or the temple. The dispute described in Amos 7:10–17 is presented in positively stylised terms, as a typical case. In this controversy between Amaziah, the 'imperial bishop' of Bethel, and Amos, the sensitive conservative from Tekoa, the point at issue was not merely Amos's criticism of the policies of the king and his ministers. What was mainly under discussion was whether, and how far, these policies were in accord with the biblical idea of God or were irreconcilable

3

with it. This, then, was a dispute about 'the truth' of talk about the God
YHWH, for whom 'the bishop' and those in power at the national sanctuary
were performing their lavish ceremonies. In the event Amos was driven out;
but for all that, his message found a place in the Old Testament collection of
books. And we see the same thing in the conflicts in which Jeremiah was
involved, or which he himself provoked.[3] How to talk about YHWH as his
people's God in a way that was true, in accordance with both his nature and
the situation of the time: this was not a marginal controversy. It was one of the
central themes in the process of passing on Israel's theological tradition.

The question was kindled especially by the phenomenon of *prophecy*.[4] The
individual opposition prophets—the so-called scriptural prophets—
reproached the priests of the sanctuary with failing in their most important
task: to seek for knowledge about God and to pass it on properly (see Hos.
4:4–6). And on the other hand these opposition prophets earned the
corresponding black marks, not only from the guild of the trained court and
temple prophets and the professional priesthood of the sanctuaries, but also
from the people who claimed religious competence because of their political
power—judgments such as 'The prophet is an imbecile, and the man of the
spirit is a madman' (Hos. 9:7), or 'What is the point of his stammering and his
blethering and his twaddle, now here, now there?' (Isa. 28:10).

The conflict about the religious competence of the various offices and their
respective holders disturbed Israel deeply and yet fascinated her. This is
evident from the numerous disputes in the history of Israel's origins passed
down to us in the canon. These read like variations on a single theme: 'Is there
a hierarchy of people responsible for the truth in Israel?' We find Aaron and
Miriam protesting against Moses's theological claims: 'Has YHWH spoken
only to Moses? Has he not spoken to us also?' (Num. 12:2). We see Korah and
his adherents—but also Eliab's sons Dathan and Abiram—rebelling against
the doctrinal and disciplinary power of Moses and Aaron: 'You claim too
much for yourselves. All the congregation are holy, every one of them, and
YHWH is among them. Why then do you set yourselves up above the
assembly of YHWH? ... Will you also play the ruler over us?' (Num. 16:3, 13).
The dispute about the right way of talking about Israel's God belongs at the
very centre of Israel's religion—as it does to the present day, incidentally.
And, as I shall try to show, everything depended—as it still does—on seeing
the dispute through, riding it out, and on drawing from it the strength for
continuing renewal.

It is certainly impossible to extract from Israel's Bible any *system* for a
particular orthodoxy, of whatever kind. And yet it may well be objected that
the process of canonisation can hardly be comprehended without the inherent
thrust towards a didactic, binding unambiguity and clarity. This may be said

in connection with the canonisation of the individual writings and of the Old Testament as a complete, self-contained book. When scholars talk about *the* theology of the book of Isaiah, or *the* theology of the Priestly Writing, they are in fact making plain the trend towards the formation of a system, by way of which—at least after the late exilic and post-exilic period—the contrary strivings of individual positions were contemplated 'as a whole' redactionally and conceptually.[5] Now doctrinal statements are formulated: YHWH is the God 'who brought (Israel) ... out of the house of bondage' (Deut. 6:12); or YHWH is 'the one God' (Deut. 6:4); or 'beside him there is no saviour' (Isa. 43:11). Now credal summaries are compiled (see Deut. 26:5–9). Now the decalogue is conceived, as a kind of Magna Carta or 'basic law' for Israel, and in Exod. 20 is put at the head of all the ethical and cultic enactments 'revealed' on Sinai. Of course these statements are the beginnings of ways of reducing talk about God to certain norms. But can we discover here the solemn claim of orthodoxy? What these statements aim to do is to cut a swathe through the thickets of tradition, and to discover focus points, so that people remain aware of 'where the path goes'.[6]

But does the Old Testament not at least have a centre, an Archimedean point so to speak, from which its many voices sound as a single voice—the voice of the one and only God who is speaking here? Is there really no recognisable and binding teaching from God, the revealer, through which, in the many faceted process of transmission, the heterodox straw can be separated from the orthodox wheat?

The answers given by scholars to this question are *controversial*. Gerhard von Rad replies with an unequivocal 'no': 'In contrast to the revelation about Christ, the Old Testament YHWH revelation is split up into a long sequence of individual acts of revelation with very varying content. It seems to lack an all-determining centre, from which the many individual acts acquire their meaning, and also the proper theological relationship to one another. We can talk about Old Testament revelation only in the sense of a multiplicity of different and varying acts of revelation.'[7] Claus Westermann's 'no' is even more uncompromising: 'The New Testament clearly has its centre in the suffering, death and resurrection of Christ. It is this towards which the gospels are aligned, and it is this from which the epistles are derived. But the structure of the Old Testament is totally different. It is therefore impossible to transfer the question about the centre of the New Testament to the Old.'[8]

Decided rejections of this kind contrast with the numerous attempts, not merely to justify the necessity and the sense of the question about a 'centre' for the Old Testament, but also to say what that centre is, and to expound it.[9] And among the supporters of theories about a 'centre' there are questions in the background which undoubtedly have to do with the theme '*orthodoxy—*

heterodoxy'. W. H. Schmidt, for example, asks: 'Which approaches and impulses are maintained through all the upheavals in the history of the tradition and in the changes of the times—especially where the relationship to God is concerned? ... Is there any fundamental concern which—explicitly or tacitly—binds together all the forms of speech and works of literature which are so different?'[10] Of course these questions themselves show that this 'centre' is not the same in kind as Christian dogma. It is not fixed by way of particular doctrinal statements. It seems to be more like a principle or axiom, which is perceived in a process of subsequent reflection. It is really no more than a 'perspective or vanishing point on which the lines converge, and which is not therefore part of the picture itself, but remains beyond it, in the picture's remoter depths'.[11] But something of *this* kind is not *palpable and at our disposal*. It actually evades every propositional definition—and is ineligible as answer to the question about orthodoxy and heterodoxy, especially when this is a question, not about a fundamental approach but about the specific form of a confession of faith.

The problem about all attempts to develop criteria of orthodoxy in the light of the biblical texts, or by way of their examination, is made radically clear by *post-biblical Judaism*, when it holds fast the mystery of the God who reveals himself on Sinai and who is beyond both orthodoxy and heterodoxy. What— the Jewish theologians continually ask—could Israel really and truly hear from the lips of its God on Sinai? Rabbi Mendel Torum of Rymanov (d. 1814), one of the great saints of Hassidism, gave the most radical answer. He said that all that Israel heard on Sinai was the consonant aleph—that hardly perceptible emission of the breath introducing the initial vowel of the personal pronoun 'anokhi, 'I', with which the biblical decalogue begins. Everything else was Moses's interpretation of that aleph. And consequently the different versions of the decalogue in Exod. 20 and Deut. 5 must also be seen as Moses's different attempts at an interpretation.[12] With this radical theory 'Rabbi Mendel Torum of Rymanov made clear ... to his contemporaries that the real and divine revelation to Israel was infinitely full of meaning, but was yet without any meaning that could be communicated. So its comprehensibility and the ability to obey what was revealed remains dependent on a profound and fundamental discernment of the tradition'.[13] The continuing, never-ending dispute about the truth of the biblical revelation is therefore rooted in that revelation itself.

Does the Old Testament tradition itself give any indication of *how this dispute ought to be carried on*? Does it offer stimuli for a theological cultivation of the dispute about the appropriate way of talking about God, beyond any suspicion of heterodoxy or heresy?

2. THE CONDITIONS OF THEOLOGICAL CONTROVERSY

Old Testament Israel knew very well how important it was to arrive at a *consensus about once-formulated texts which were an authentic expression of Yahweh's acts towards Israel.* These texts were preserved and passed on from generation to generation—but they were also continually enriched and interwoven with new material.[14] The Old Testament's literary and theological complexity is not merely an external feature. It is constitutive for Israel's dealings with the truth. Norbert Lohfink has therefore rightly termed Israel 'a learning community'.[15] But the many forms of learning (text-orientated: see Deut. 6:4–9; 32:1–43; situation-orientated: see Deut. 6:21–25; group-orientated: see Deut. 31:10–13) are not primarily concerned with passing on canonised teaching. *Putting what has been learnt to the test in the everyday life of society is the main stress.* What is put into Moses's mouth in Deut. 32:45–47 is the basic perspective of the whole biblical transmission process: 'Lay to heart all these enactments. Today I enjoin you: Command your children, that they too may be careful to keep all the precepts of this teaching. This is not empty word without importance for you, but it is your life. If you keep this word you shall live long in the land which you are going over the Jordan to possess.' Israel's learning is 'learning life', and whatever has to be learnt (and taught) in Israel must be legitimated by its capacity for increasing life (see also Deut. 4:40; 6:24; 30:15–20, especially 30:9). For *Israel doctrine and life are bound together in a productive correlation.* What is supposed to be taught and learnt has to do with successful living.[16] And since life exists and takes its course in historical and social contexts, the same may be said about the *Word of 'the teaching':* 'It is not in heaven, so that you would have to say: "Who will go up for us to heaven, and bring it down and proclaim it to us, so that we may do it?" Neither is it beyond the sea, so that you would have to say: "Who will go over the sea for us, and bring it to us and proclaim it to us, so that we may do it?" No, the word is very near you; it is in your mouth and in your heart, you can do it' (Deut. 30:11–14). The Word proves itself in the absolutely endless, protean forms of life, and in that life it continually acquires new nuances, which are then gathered together and passed on. What was not foreseeable yesterday can be important today, and tomorrow can once more recede into the background. But it is not forgotten. It is *aufgehoben*, in all the senses in which Hegel used the word: abolished, but only in so far as it is preserved and gathered up into something further—here as an offer of teaching and learning for further living.[17]

If we wish to talk at all about orthodoxy in the formation of Israel's tradition, we might perhaps term it a *kairological orthodoxy in dialogue form.* Israel knows the three constituents which are summed up in this concept.

(a) Without its ties with what preceding generations taught and learnt, Israel would be without a home and a foundation (see Deut. 32:45–47). (b) So that Israel could receive its social and political life from its God's hand in the fullest sense, continual new attempts were made to formulate what had been passed down about God in a way that was related to the present situation, so that the 'today' of this language (see Deut. 5.24: Ps. 95.7) was comprehensible and part of contemporary experience. (c) Israel allows these many different attempts to stand side by side unharmonised in its Bible; and this must be interpreted as an offer of dialogue—certainly not an offer of the kind made by a mail-order catalogue, but an offer intended as an encouragement to 'choose life' (see Deut. 30:19). That is to say, it was an encouragement to find *one's own* Word and to put it to the test. This kairological orthodoxy in dialogue form is backed by 'the sober theological insight that a revelation that stands in the way of successful living cannot be "true"; ultimately, its truth is decided by its relevance, its practical value in achieving "successful life" ...'[18] And according to the Old Testament perspective 'successful life' means life fulfilled in the community of the people and with God.[19]

But if Old Testament orthodoxy is kairological and dialogistic, this principle resists the naive thesis, so cherished among Christians, about a *qualitatively progressive revelation*, whereby texts later in time replace and supersede those that have gone before. This pattern of thinking is very popular, at least in defining the relationship between the Old Testament and the New. *We meet it in two variations.* The first is a somewhat simple-minded, popularised version, which feels able to maintain that 'increased refinement can be detected in the Old Testament', and that 'what we find at a lower level in the Old Testament, striving upwards in its crude way, then appears in pure and spiritualised form in the New.'[20] The other variation is the product of theological reflection, and is at first sight impressive, since it establishes an actual ontological connection between the Old and New Testaments. The Old Testament stream of tradition thrusts consistently forward into the New, and finds its completion there.[21] These two variations agree in maintaining that, for the New Testament faith, what the Old Testament has to say has ultimately a merely anticipatory and provisional, historical validity—which means that for us contemporary people, it has in the last resort no validity at all.

Both variations are not merely historically false and theologically unacceptable, as far as the relation of the two testaments is concerned.[22] They are wrong even within the confines of the Old Testament itself. Who would seriously maintain that the Priestly Writing is 'progressive revelation' compared with the Yahwist's narrative? The Priestly Writing is neither conceived as 'improvement' nor is it comprehensible in that light. Its 'orthodoxy' cannot be judged according to the yardstick of higher or lower, but *only according to the kairos in which it was written and accepted*—and in whose light it proves its 'utility' for life today also, or for life in the future, according to the particular constellation of society and the times. And who would actually maintain that the timid reaction of the epilogue to the Book of Ecclesiastes is theologically the 'better' or 'truer', when we read: 'My son, beware! Of making of many books there is no end, and much study is a weariness to the flesh. If you have heard it all (i.e., and read what is written in this book) the conclusion is: Fear God, and keep his commandments. This is all a person needs. For God will bring every deed into judgment, where everything hidden will be judged, whether it is good or evil' (Eccles. 12:12–14). But it is precisely the orthodox simplicity of the epilogue's slogan 'fear God and keep his commandments' that Ecclesiastes is fighting against! Yet the biblical tradition preserves *both* positions—simply as the offer of an orthodoxy in dialogue which makes decision possible, and encourages it.

Something similar emerges from many texts and in connection with numerous themes, from the dialogistic structure of the two creation theologies in Gen. 1 and Gen. 2, down to the prophetic-apocalyptic visions of the end, or completion, of history. Or we may think of the enthusiastic affirmation of human existence in Ps. 8 over against Job 7's complete rejection of the very anthropology that Ps. 8 maintains (compare Job 7:17f. with Ps. 8.4), to say nothing of the directly contradictory commentaries on the institution of the monarchy, the temple and the sacrificial cult.[23] That Israel should have canonised the whole range of 'teaching' in its sacred scriptures emphasises the seriousness with which it accepted the *kairoi* of its history and its life from the hand of its God. And even more does it show the commitment which Israel required of itself: *the dispute about the truth, which must never be ended by any answers that have been once discovered.*

Of course in this dispute there are *guardians of tradition and official interpreters*. And there are individuals who blaze fresh trails, who are neither the one nor the other, but who fought against both. But *all* these groups were forced to struggle for one thing: the *assent of the people*. Often this was achieved late enough—in the case of some of the prophets, only after centuries.[24] But without this acceptance there is no canonical orthodoxy. This remained true down to the period when the canon was definitively fixed. The book of Ecclesiastes—even the book of Ezekiel—stood in striking tension to important basic assertions of the Torah. Yet they were finally none the less permitted to remain in the canon of Holy Scripture, because the majority of the rabbis at Jabneh (at the end of the first century AD) were in favour of their retention.[25]

In the Old Testament, therefore, *orthodoxy had to be an orthodoxy accepted by the majority*. This is made especially plain by two groups of linked concepts.

On the one hand, we continually come across the idea that 'teachings' are put to the assembled people for their 'choice', so that they can agree freely (Exod. 19:7f.; 24:3; Deut. 33; Josh. 24). The God of the Bible does not want slaves, without the capacity for free decision, or easy-going bureaucrats of his Word. He wants comprehending and assenting, free, conscious subjects, who know what they say and what they do. The other group of concepts trusts the power of the divine Spirit, which makes testimony and teaching possible—even without any official teaching body or ministry. That is one of the main assertions in the vision of the new convenant in Jer. 31:31–34. No one needs to teach anyone else, or may do so, because God takes the role of teacher upon himself.

The confidence of Old Testament Jewish tradition that the God of the Bible guides the majority in the direction of kairological, dialogistic orthodoxy, is summed up by a well known story from the Babylonian Talmud.[26] In one of the Palestinian schools, round about 100 AD, the two authorities Rabbi Eliezer and Rabbi Joshua were, as often before, unable to agree, in spite of intense discussion. A vote was therefore taken in the rabbinic assembly, and it emerged that everyone believed that Rabbi Joshua's position was correct. Only one person voted for Rabbi Eliezer's view—himself! He then had recourse to spectacular miracles, and even challenged God in heaven to declare his own opinion. But neither the miracles nor the divine voice could convince the assembly. The story explains why: 'On that day R. Eliezer brought forward every imaginable argument, but they did not accept them. Said he to them: "If the *halachah* agrees with me, let this carob-tree prove it!" Thereupon the carob-tree was torn a hundred cubits out of its place—others affirm, four hundred cubits. "No proof can be brought from a carob-tree," they retorted. Again he said to them: "If the *halachah* agrees with me, let the stream of water prove it!" Whereupon the stream of water flowed backwards. "No proof can be brought from a stream of water," they rejoined. Again he urged: "If the *halachah* agrees with me, let the walls of the schoolhouse prove it," whereupon the walls inclined to fall. But R. Joshua rebuked them, saying: "When scholars are engaged in a *halachic* dispute, what have ye to interfere?" Hence they did not fall, in honour of R. Joshua, nor did they resume the upright, in honour of R. Eliezer; and they are still standing thus inclined. Again he said to them: "If the *halachah* agrees with me, let it be proved from Heaven!" Whereupon a Heavenly Voice cried out: "Why do ye dispute with R. Eliezer, seeing that in all matters the *halachah* agrees with him!" But R. Joshua arose and exclaimed "*It is not in heaven*" (Deut. 30:12). What did he mean by this? Said R. Jeremiah: "That the Torah had already been given at Mount Sinai; we pay no attention to a Heavenly Voice, because Thou has long since written in the Torah at Mount Sinai, *After the majority must one incline*" (Exod. 23:2).

'R. Nathan met Elijah and asked him: What did the Holy One, Blessed be He, do in that hour?—He laughed [with joy], he replied, saying, "My sons have defeated Me, My sons have defeated Me." '

Neither miracle nor recourse to the citation of a divine Word support orthodoxy, but only the assenting perception that the truth of a doctrinal statement is backed up by the people's experience. In the Old Testament there is *no separation between orthodoxy and orthopraxis*.

3. THE THEOLOGICAL DIGNITY OF PRAXIS

If I nevertheless go on to talk about a *'hierarchical' order among the different parts of the Old Testament*, this implies no modification of what I have said about the many-faceted form of the Old Testament. It is not meant to be a reversion to the thesis about a canon within the canon. But at the same time it must be stressed that the *final canonical form of the Old Testament is a hermeneutical guideline*—the parameter of orthodoxy, so to speak. All the different views about the inner structure of the Old Testament in the later Old Testament period, in the New Testament texts, in the first centuries of post-biblical Judaism, and in post-biblical Christianity,[27] agree about one thing: the canon is divided up into three parts, which reflect a theological system of co-ordinates. To put it simply, the order of the books in the canon of the Greek Bible can be understood as a triple movement: 'the foundation of history' (= the narrative books); the 'present' (= the psalms and the wisdom books); 'the future as the completion of history' (= the prophetic books). The canon of the Hebrew Bible is different since it divides into the Torah (= the Pentateuch); the prophets (Josh. – II Kings + the prophetic books); the writings (= the other, relatively late books). In this final form the systematic precedence of the Torah emerges in several ways. (a) The Torah unfolds the indissoluble dialectic of history and law, though the broad centring on the law in the middle of the books Genesis to Deuteronomy (the second half of Exod., the whole book of Lev. and the first half of Num.) shows that the main stress is on the practical application. (b) The prophetic books are related to the Torah, understood in this sense. They interpret the Torah, keep it from becoming fossilised, and extend it into the present—thus emphasising that the Torah is something to be 'done' and 'lived'. (c) 'The writings' are more loosely linked with the Torah, thematically and in origin. But they are nevertheless a collection of attempts to show how life in the everyday world can be mastered with the help of Torah and prophets.

This structure makes it clear that *in the light of the Hebrew canon praxis— practical living—is the place where theory is decided*, develops and proves itself.

It is true that the history of God's own commitment is at the beginning of it all. But this history comes together in concentrated form in the law, which thrusts towards practical application, in order once more to make history possible.[28]

For Israel, then, orthodoxy can only emerge, 'take flesh' and be properly apprehended in orthopraxis. This fact is especially registered and thought about in the *stories that tell about a direct confrontation between YHWH and a single individual, or a whole people.*

The very beginning of the Abraham stories emphasises that the biblical God sends a person on his way and encounters him on that way. Abraham 'sees' God (Gen. 12:7: YHWH 'appeared'—i.e., allowed himself to be seen) only after he had obeyed the exhortation: 'Go away from the country where you have been up to now to the land that I will show you ... (Gen. 12:1). And the promise of blessing 'in you/through you all the families of the earth shall receive blessing ...' (Gen. 12:3) *also* means that blessing comes to all those who, like Abraham and following in his steps, allow their (new) existence to be given to them by the biblical God.[29]

This is a painful, irksome way of living, because it requires conversion, or a new direction. That is the leading theological idea of the narrative cycle about Jacob (Gen. 25–36). In this series of stories, Israel talks about herself, about the metamorphosis demanded and given by God, through which she thrusts through to her real, authentic identity. What the mysterious man says at the river Jabbok in the night sums up the theme of the cycle: 'Your name shall no more be called Jacob, but Israel' (Gen. 32:28). How this comes about, and what it means in concrete terms, is related in the individual stories gathered together in Genesis 25 to 36. Here are drawn for us all conceivable constellations, confusions and entanglements of human existence in the warp and weft of love and labour, trickery and egotism, helplessness and arrogance, fear, rivalry and hate. Religion is not lacking either. But it is only in that night at the Jabbok that the true dimension of the biblical idea of God becomes evident, when God himself challenges Jacob to the contest. For the mystery of the biblical God is revealed only to the person who allows himself to be encountered, and indeed wounded, by that God—as Jacob 'learnt' at the Jabbok. It is true that, in his usual manner, he tries to escape his own metamorphosis by asking the mysterious stranger for *his* identity and *his* legitimation (Gen. 32:29: 'Tell me, I pray, your name'). But he is given no reply. What is demanded is *a different* answer, the person's admission of *his own* identity, before God and with him: 'What is your name?' that is, do you really know who you are? (Gen. 32:27). And when Jacob answers 'I am Jacob', this is the confession that releases the tension: 'You shall no longer be Jacob but Israel, for you have entered into a struggle with God' (Gen. 32:28).

Now the die has been cast: the old Jacob, Jacob the trickster, the Jacob who measured life against his own requirements, his own power and his own success—always at the cost of other people, even at God's cost—this Jacob no longer exists. His encounter with God has transformed him. He emerges from it a new person, a person who has at long last come to himself, even if only under compulsion. Now he has been blessed—and also wounded: when the night is past, Jacob is lame in one hip. From a struggle like this, when a person is confronted by his God, no one ends up as he began. But the pain of this newly created Israel recedes in the face of the new experience: 'The sun rose upon him' (Gen. 32:31). Now the world and his own life—and his God—all look different: 'So Jacob called the name of the place Peniel, saying, "For I have seen God face to face, and my life was preserved" ' (Gen. 32:30). Now he has learnt *how* this God saves, and *whom* he saves: *he saves through conversion and renewal.* And that is why the story has to continue. It is really only now that it moves towards its proper climax. Biblical experience of God is not ended by a new experience of one's own self. It is complete in the new experience of the other, and of others. The ancient story-tellers have set the meeting between the two brothers, Esau and Jacob, which now follows (Gen. 33:1–16), in subtle parallel to the story about the meeting between Jacob and his God in the night.[30] The correspondence indicated through the narrative is obvious in substance. Having all his life played the role of the man who is always triumphantly successful, the new Jacob-Israel now throws himself at his brother's feet. And then it happens. The one cheated runs to meet the cheat who begs for forgiveness. He embraces him and they weep. For the first time they address one another as 'my brother' (Gen. 33:9). Jacob says finally that in Esau, the forgiving brother, he sees the face of God. *Jacob only realises who this God YHWH really is when he acts as this God acts*—discovering in the process that to do so makes new life possible.

Only those who follow *God's* ways can know and 'see' God: this is the great theme of the Sinai traditions.[31] When Moses asks to look upon God's glory and to know *his* ways, his first petition is rejected, but his second is granted: 'You cannot see my face ... But I will let my glory pass by you ... And I will cover you with my hand (concealing myself and protecting you) while I pass by you. Then I will take away my hand, and you shall see my back' (Exod. 33:20–23). This answer certainly stresses the dialectic of the God who comes near and who is in that very approach the God who also distances himself. The self-revealing God is in his unveiling always at once the God who conceals himself. But another dimension echoes in the answer too, the back of another person is seen best by the one who goes behind, who follows him. This is true of the person who pursues the paths which the God who passes over in Exod. 34:6f. describes: 'YHWH is a merciful and gracious El [God], slow to anger, abounding in steadfast love and faithfulness. He keeps steadfast love for thousands, forgiving entanglement in guilt, rebellions and transgression. But he is not indifferent towards sin: he visits the guilt of the fathers upon their sons and grandchildren, to the third and fourth generation.' *This* is the way to which he calls Moses and his people. *This* is the way that has to be taken, if the secret of the God of Sinai is to be comprehended. The person who can really grasp and understand who this God is, is the person who—weary and entangled in guilt—seeks the strength to go forward through the cry for YHWH's forgiveness. It is the person who himself forgives, as this God forgives, who is himself immeasurably kind, as God is immeasurably kind— just as, and just because, this is the path on which the God of the Bible precedes us.

The mystery of this God is not revealed in the contemplation or cultivation of a picture of him, however beautiful; nor is it revealed in the invocation of a doctrinal tenet, however true. *It is revealed when we take the path to which he calls:* 'You stood at the foot of the mountain and the mountain burned: fire to the heart of heaven, darkness, clouds and gloom. YHWH spoke to you out of the midst of the fire. You heard the thunder of the words. A form you did not see. You heard only the thunder. YHWH revealed to you his covenant, he commanded you to perform it: the Ten Words' (Deut. 4:11–13). It is in doing the Ten Words and by doing them that we learn who the God of Sinai is.

Orthodoxy is determined and purged by orthopraxis. This is also the quintessence of all prophetic interventions, which can be summed up in the words of Micah 6.8: 'You have been told, O man, what is good and what YHWH expects of you. Nothing other than this: to do justice, to love kindness and faithfulness, to walk in reverence with your God.'

Translated Margaret Kohl

Notes

1. E. Brunner *Revelation and Reason*, trans. O. Wyon (London 1947). The quotation has been translated directly from the German edition (*Offenbarung und Vernunft*, Zürich 1941) p. 287.

2. G. von Rad 'Offene Fragen im Umkreis einer Theologie des Alten Testaments' *Theologische Literaturzeitung* 88 (1963) 405.

3. See especially the conflicts with Pashhur (Jer. 20:1–6) and Hananiah (Jer. 27–28), but also with the kings Jehoiakim (Jer. 36) and Zedekiah (Jer. 37–38).

4. See the instructive survey in F. L. Hossfeld and I. Meyer *Prophet gegen Prophet. Eine Analyse alttestamentlicher Texte zum Thema: Wahre und falsche Propheten* (Fribourg 1973).

5. The deuteronomistic editings of the historical traditions and the prophetic

books should be especially remembered here; but we may also think of the final edited form of the Pentateuch.

6. See here R. Smend 'Theologie im Alten Testament' in his *Die Mitte des Alten Testaments. Gesammelte Studien* I (Munich 1986) pp. 111–115.

7. G. von Rad *Old Testament Theology*, trans. D. M. G. Stalker, I (London 1962). The quotation has been translated directly from the German edition (*Theologie des Alten Testaments* I, 5° Munich 1966) pp. 128f.

8. C. Westermann *Theologie des Alten Testaments in Grundzügen* (Göttingen 1978) p. 5.

9. See the survey and suggestions in the work of Smend cited in note 6, pp. 40–84; also G. F. Hasel 'The Problem of the Center in the OT Theology Debate' *Zeitschrift für Alttestamentliche Wissenschaft* 86 (1974) 65–82; E. Zenger 'Die Mitte der alttestamentlichen Glaubensgeschichte' *Katechetische Blätter* 101 (1976) 3–16.

10. W. H. Schmidt 'Die Frage nach der "Mitte" des Alten Testaments im Spannungsfeld von Religionsgeschichte und Theologie' in K. Jürgensen, *Gott loben das ist unser Amt* F. O. Scharbau and W. H. Schmidt (eds.) (Kiel 1984) pp. 55–65.

11. W. Zimmerli 'Zum Problem der "Mitte des Alten Testaments" ' *Evangelische Theologie* 25 (1975) 103.

12. See here especially F. L. Hossfeld *Der Dekalog. Seine späten Fassungen, die originale Komposition und seine Vorstufen* (Fribourg, Göttingen 1982).

13. K. Müller 'Biblische Begriffe in jüdischer Sicht' *Christ in der Gegenwart* 37 (1985) 111.

14. The Old Testament is consequently a literary compilation, not of authors but of traditions.

15. N. Lohfink 'Gottesvolk als Lerngemeinschaft' *Bibel und Kirche* (1984) 90–100.

16. See G. von Rad's profound remarks in *Wisdom in Israel*, trans. J. D. Martin (London 1972).

17. W. Zimmerli introduced the concept of *Fortschreibung* ('prolongation') for this procedure. See especially his 'Das Phänomen der "Fortschreibung" im Buche Ezechiel' in *Prophecy. Essays Presented to G. Fohrer*, ed. J. A. Emerton (Berlin, New York 1980) pp. 174–191; also recently C. Levin *Die Verheißung des neuen Bundes* (Göttingen 1985) pp. 162–165.

18. Müller, the article cited in note 13, p. 15.

19. See here E. Zenger 'Erfahrung-Weisheit-Weisung. Zur Struktur biblisch-appellativer Texte' in *Ethische Predigt und Alltagsverhalten* eds. F. Kamphaus and R. Zerfaß (Munich, Mainz 1977) pp. 29–43.

20. Still the formulation (appallingly!) in the Dutch catechism (German edition Freiburg 1969 pp. 69, 71).

21. Thus for example H. Gese 'Erwägungen zur Einheit der biblischen Theologie' *Zeitschrift für Theologie und Kirche* 67 (1970) 417–436.

22. For criticism see among others H. D. Preuß *Das Alte Testament in christlicher Predigt* (Stuttgart 1984); M. Oeming *Gesamtbiblische Theologien der Gegenwart. Das Verhältnis von AT und NT in der hermeneutischen Diskussion seit Gerhard von Rad* (Stuttgart 1985).

23. See W. H. Schmidt 'Vielfalt und Einheit alttestamentlichen Glaubens' in '*Wenn nicht jetzt, wann dann?*'. *Aufsätze für Hans-Joachim Kraus*, ed. H.-G. Geyer *et al* (Neukirchen 1983) p. 14.

24. As 'people's book' the Old Testament is as far as I know a unique phenomenon in the history of ancient oriental literature.

25. This did not come about in a 'synod', however, as is often said, but through the crystallisation of a consensus; see here especially P. Schäfer 'Die sogenannte Synode von Jabne. Zur Trennung von Juden und Christen im ersten/zweiten Jh. n. Chr.' *Judaica* 31 (1975) 54–64, 116–124.

26. See *The Babylonian Talmud*. *Baba Mezi'a* (bBM 59a–59b), this portion trans. into English by H. Freedman (1935) pp. 352f. See also Müller, the article cited in note 13, at pp. 79 and 95.

27. It is impossible to describe in detail here the complex historical process whereby the canon and the canonical structures of the Hebrew, Greek and Latin traditions were arrived at, but an examination shows that the theory of a 'completed' revelation presents considerable difficulties!

28. The law/gospel or gospel/law alternatives are therefore gross simplifications.

29. See here E. Zenger 'Jahwe, Abraham und das Heil aller Völker' in *Absolutheit des Christentums* ed. W. Kasper (Freiburg 1977) pp. 39–62.

30. G. von Rad *Genesis, A Commentary*, trans. J. H. Marks, revised ed. (London 1972).

31. See here E. Zenger *Israel am Sinai, Analysen und Interpretationen zu Exodus 17–34*, (2° Altenberge 1985).

André Paul

The Structural Supports of Orthodoxy in the Jewish System and the Christian System

WE SHALL be attempting in this article to present the reasons for and the fact of orthodoxy, against a backcloth description of the social-doctrinal systems of Judaism and Christianity respectively.

By *Judaism* and *Christianity* we mean *two realities*, the Jewish and the Christian, which came into being together and symmetrically at the end of the first century of our era. They are non-identical twins, born of the ambiguous thing that lived for centuries and which we call, not Judaism, but 'proto-Judaism' or 'proto-Christianity' according to context.

Two social, ideological and doctrinal coherencies or systems grew up, on the surface very similar but fundamentally irreconcilable in their essential difference.

Is *orthodoxy* necessary and possible in each of the two systems? If so, what conditions does it require and what effects does it have? Those are the questions we shall be attempting to answer in this article.

1. JUDAISM IN ITS COHERENCE AND SYSTEM

(a) The destiny of a nation of exiles

Judaism, as we know, was first organised and established and then defined on the ruins of the Temple of Jerusalem, after 70. From then on it had a unique and specific relation with that Temple: being founded on an absence *that relation was symbolic and even mythic.* The absence was that of a concrete institution, which for many years had been the necessary centre of a religious and political system. The centre was the basis on which the Judaic authorities had united the constituent populations, those of the national land and the Diaspora.

The existence of the Diaspora presupposes distance: distance from the national land but above all distance from the one Temple, the guarantor of the survival of national values. Diaspora causes and even requires the traditional religious heritage to be relatively but adequately open to the local language and culture. And with diaspora comes pilgrimage.

The disappearance of the Temple and even more the disappearance of a Jewish land with independent status destroyed by their very occurrence the conditions in which a national diaspora could exist. But more than that, they made it necessary to establish on firm foundations a different kind of organisation, that of *Exile*[1]. And this is a very different matter. The Temple had been the topographical and ideological centre of the national and religious integration and cohesion functions. And exile was the political, social and national result of the disappearance of that centre. From then on, with the advent of exile, the individual's and therefore the group's identity can persist only through exclusive recognition of the national moral and cultural heritage, every particular of which is to be preserved. Whereas in diaspora any language may be the mother tongue and therefore varied, and any land may be one's country,[2] in exile communication and complicity with one's surroundings will not go beyond conceding the minimum of social relations and exchanges needed to ensure general subsistance. And whereas in diaspora a man will be truly at home away from the national land, the exile nourishes in himself and others awareness that he is a 'stranger'.[3] And again, whereas in diaspora men make the pilgrimage to the Temple of Jerusalem as if they were just going on a trip abroad, the exile cannot cease thinking of it as, wishing it to be, and even seeing it in the light of a return to his country of origin and only true home.

Since 70, it is thus as a *group and religion of exile*, in other words as a *nation of exiles*, that Judaism henceforth exists and only can exist.

(b) Adam, the first Jew and the first man

For the Jew, the national land, which is physically lost but symbolically saved, is the *archetypal land*; from this land sprang his earliest ancestor, Adam in person, who awaits him there. In the traditional Judaic system, the first man was truly Jewish, and his exclusive language, Hebrew. True, the Talmud teaches us that the dust Adam was made from was 'collected from the whole world'; it specifies however that the head of the first man was formed with 'earth of Israel'. There have been attempts to identify the—logically unique— place from which the earth used in creating Adam came. Some texts speak of a 'pure place which is the navel of the earth'. It is often called 'the site of the Temple' or of 'the Sanctuary', and from the second century BC up to Rashi (1040–1105) this lovely tradition is widely repeated.[4] More, the belief that at the moment of death every man's body returns to the earth it came from was systematised to the point of being applied to the first man himself. As early as 150 BC, the *Book of Jubilees* tells us that when Adam died, 'his children buried him in the country of the creation' (IV,29). And it will even be specified that 'Adam was created from the place of his expiation'. This teaching on the national and cultic origin of the first man is in practice an established one among Jews and is extremely important. Its *sacrificial dimension* is reinforced elsewhere; as early as the first century of our era, Flavius Josephus states that the mount (Moriah) of the Sacrifice of Isaac is none other than the mount of the Temple, and this interpretation is found again later in the *Targum of the Pentateuch*. The ancient Jews had made a direct connection between the person of Adam and this same mount Moriah. According to several sources God settled him there immediately after the Fall.

A whole system of doctrine is thus conveyed by this myth cycle with the Temple as its centre and Adam, who is both the first man and the first Jew, as its sole figure. The Temple is linked with the Creation of the earliest man, but also to his redemption after the Fall, to his death and even his burial.

(c) The mythic function of the Hebrew language

There is another characteristic connected with the Adam-Temple pair—a structurally Jewish pair, we should stress—and that is the use of Hebrew alone.

In rabbinic teaching—which is to say in the traditions found collected in the Talmud, the Targumim and the Midrashim—plurality of languages is an empirical fact which must be considered in relation to plurality of peoples. But it should primarily be situated in relation to the use of the *one language*, i.e. Hebrew, the only language to exist until the Babel disaster. This one language is presented by the Jews as the 'holy language'; as the texts make abundantly clear, this means the language of the Creation, of the Sanctuary or the Temple, of answerable prayer, of heavenly beings and also of all living things on earth before Babel, including the animals (for example the serpent speaking to Eve in the garden of Eden). According to the same traditions this language, immortal and still possessed of its original virtues and inalienable qualities, still exists and will continue to exist, whatever happens to or in the history of mankind. In this language too the gift of the Torah was made at Sinai. Hebrew is thus seen both as antedating the history of the world and of man, including the salvific relation of human history to its divine principle, and as posterior to it. For Hebrew is the language of God, of Adam, and of the Jewish nation.

Given their situation as a nation in exile, the Jews were obliged to institutionalise and proclaim the sacred function and mythic power of Hebrew in various ways. The heavenly and the national dimensions found a natural shared ground in it. So the two preeminent functions, of land and language, come together to form the central axis of the Jewish doctrinal synthesis founded on this central principle: Adam, the first man, was the first Jew; and God, the Creator and Revealer, has no language but Adam's, which is the language of the Jews. Thus *nation, land* and *language* form three fundamental concepts in the teaching of the rabbis. There is a fourth one, that of *Torah*.

(d) The role of infinite revelation

The most important word in Judaism is 'Torah', meaning 'Doctrine'. It only gradually became established with this exact meaning, having originally only really referred to what we call the Pentateuch. But later, when the Jews had almost finished elaborating their ethical and doctrinal system, it came to mean the whole corpus of their sacred writings, i.e. the twenty or so biblical books or *Written Torah*, and, under the name *Oral Torah*, the *Mishnah*, which had boldly appeared in about 200, with its peripheral or derivative literature: the tosefta or 'complement', the *Palestinian Talmud* and *Babylonian Talmud*, and the great collections of biblical commentaries, known as *Midrashim*. The appearance of the code of the Mishnah, it should be pointed out, was a literary event of immense importance for the Jews, and had a profound and dramatic effect on the community. Nothing like it had happened for many years, except for the doctrine taught by Jesus and spread by the gospels. The limits and even the nature of the established corpus of their Scriptures was opened up and brought into question. There now appeared a hitherto unknown literary space which, once the Mishnah had opened it up, not only failed to close but grew steadily more voracious. Thus the space became a place in which were erected literary, doctrinal and social constructs of permanent and basic importance for the Jewish nation. The Palestinian Talmud, the first commentary on the Mishnah, was the first to appear, in the third and fourth centuries; then from the fifth century onward came the Babylonian Talmud and the Midrashim. It could be said that the Jews' New Testament was born. And what had taken shape was a *four-sided literary-doctrinal structure in which interpretation and interpreted fuse into a single entity*: in the Torah, the Talmud is to the Mishnah as the Midrashim are to Scripture. Here, irreversibly and completely, Judaism had the perfect structure without which it could no longer live. And this perfect structure is the *Torah*.[5]

In the Torah, each element has the same status. A totalising intertextuality runs through all the literary divisions; integration is brought about by the logic of revelation itself. But this revelation is infinite and unceasingly in act, today, yesterday, tomorrow.

(e) The immortal Temple of the Torah

Several rabbinic documents assert and Judaism traditionally teaches that the Torah was given or 'revealed' to Moses at Sinai. Judaism, it must be stated, rests in large part on the established existence of rabbis. Now, both in antiquity and later, every rabbi is in some sense the ideal model legislator Moses; he has also the faculty of being himself an agent in the as it were endless process of sinaitic revelation. It should be remembered that Judaism is the religion, the doctrine and in a way the culture of a group without national land, Temple or State—dispossessed, in other words, of the whole set of things and institutions which any ancient political apparatus needed to exist. If it is to survive under these conditions, the group needs hope, and to that end first of all needs cohesion and doctrine. For this group Moses is not the charismatic leader bringing the Hebrews out of Egypt but the complete and perfect rabbi. The God of Israel for his part, or just plain God, ceases to be the Conquering Warrior and takes on the exclusive features of the Supreme Rabbi. And the revealed and revealing Torah replaces the Temple as the necessary place and possible time of God's self-revelation.

Hic et nunc, it is the rabbi's task to be the mediator of a revelation we have said is always in act. He assumes this task as a continuer of Moses' work at Sinai. He is not a priest for there is no Temple, but he has a kind of literary-doctrinal priesthood. In his so to speak mythic mediation of the Sinai event, he compensates in the here and now for the lack of a temple. Hence the need for a sacred language, officially known as the 'language of the Sanctuary'.

Thanks to the Torah, which is 'Doctrine', and even exhaustive doctrine, and thanks to the Torah alone, it is made possible for Judaism, a social-religious entity fundamentally different from any other, to maintain its essential limits. Scripture and Doctrine (or to use Christian terms, Faith—in the objective sense of course), or alternatively Scripture and Tradition are fused in the Torah, whose constituents have mythic effects. Through these effects the Jew can at any time and in any place, immediately and as it were magically, sacramentally one could say, transport himself from the so-called pagan land in which he is obliged to live. In this way he is 'sanctified', in a Temple which this time is immortal, for it is an endless reservoir of inexhaustible words of revelation.

2. CHRISTIANITY AND THE COHERENCE OF THE JEWISH SYSTEM

(a) The fortunes of a scattered people

Whereas Judaism was organised as a social-doctrinal system of exile, Christianity is the literary and social heir of the diaspora. It may even be said moreover—and rightly as we shall show—that the diaspora quality and function are essentially constitutive of the centre and driving force of Christianity.

For Christianity, unlike Judaism, *does have the Temple*: the mythic and therefore unique Temple first of all, 'the Temple of his body' according to John 2:21 which refers solely to Christ; but also the actual temple of the cult, with, on the one hand, the physical institution of the *hieron* throughout the so-called Christian world, and, on the other, its well-known *hierarchical organisation*. There is, putting it bluntly, no such thing as a Christian land or Christian lands: there are just Christians, who are scattered round the world like elements in a vast and limitless *Diaspora* (*diaspora* is a Greek word meaning 'dispersion, scattering'). We said earlier that diaspora presupposes a single Temple, and at least some degree of openness in the religious heritage to the local language and culture. Since 70 these conditions cannot obtain for the Jews; they only exist now in Christianity, always provided one accepts that the formula 'the Temple of his body'—which corresponds among Christians to the Jewish 'Torah given at Sinai'—functionally designates the one true Temple. It should be added that Christians have their 'Holy Land', which they have always made pilgrimages to from the beginning and for which, at least in the middle ages, they have been ready to take up arms. But in no sense is it a national land, an *Erez Israel*, as it is for the Jews. Moreover, the tomb they go on pilgrimage to is physically there, unlike the burial-place of Adam, which belongs to the ideological-mythic system by means of which the Jews prove the uniqueness of their status, not only among men but in the whole universe too.

For the Christian, as was the case of the Jew Philo of Alexandria, any inhabited land is a true 'homeland'. The Christian, belonging to *diaspora*, is a member of an *ecclesia*, an 'assembly';—and there must first be 'dispersal' if there is to be 'assembly'. Diaspora is therefore for the Christian not only rightful but also necessary. And it can be said that '*diaspora*' *is the first concept that can be suggested to describe the Christian system*. It immediately positions the social dimension of Christianity on its relevant axis, and it conditions the choice and suitable description of the other dimensions.

It is therefore as a *diaspora group* and *diaspora religion*, in other words as a *scattered people* (not *nation* like the Jews), that Christianity has from the start existed and only can exist.

(b) The cultural vocation of Christianity

Another great difference between Jews and Christians is that just as they have no national land, so Christians have no holy language.

Whereas in Judaism, as we have shown, the linguistic dimension or function is centripetal, in Christianity it is centrifugal. Any language through which the so-called Christian Bible or Scripture, Doctrine, and culture are expressed is 'holy'. Here again, the Christians followed on from the Jews of the Diaspora, who with the Septuagint and the vast amount of accompanying Greek-language literature had positively brought about a real *cultural conversion*. There can only be diaspora if a conversion of this kind follows and completes social implantation. The result of this process, to be seen both among Jews of the diaspora before Christ and in the history of Christianity, is that any fully recognised translation has initiated and promoted a general literary and cultural movement. So it is important to observe the cultural effect of translations of the Bible, since their strictly literary impact is accompanied by wider phenomena, most striking in the field of the arts, plastic, musical and others, including the most recent. To take just the Bible from the specific Christian inheritance, one can say that it only exists and lives in Christianity thanks to the concurrence of several forms of expression. To a certain extent, limits of which are those of the canon itself as we shall be saying, these various forms of expression themselves contribute to the translation of the Bible. There is also the ethical dimension of social discourse which is inevitably marked by the spread of the Bible, and many other facts which, when they are linked and assembled, go to build and make manifest what is called a culture, and in the longer term a civilisation.

It must not be forgotten that in the cultural conversion-production that is characteristic of the diaspora person and therefore *a fortiori* of the Christian, receiving necessarily goes along with giving. Christianity is marked by the world but itself marks the world. Thus, in differing degrees depending on time and place, large areas or large stretches of the Christian world can be identified by their dominant original culture. Now—to resume our theme—so wide and strong is the power of a translation like the Vulgate that at certain points in history a Jewish-style 'sacred language' seems to be coming into being. This is rather what happened with Latin in western Christianity until the 1960s. But the very dynamic of the institutions and the group involved always proved capable of restoring the correct perspective, that of a *vulgate of vulgates rather than some fixed and tyranical Vulgate.* And further, the diaspora status of Christianity of itself reasserted the difference between Christian ideology and the ideology behind the Jewish doctrine of the 'holy language'. The object and finality of this doctrine are such that Judaism has not once in the course of its history given rise to a culture properly so-called: its status as an exile group and exile religion diverted it away from or totally prevented it from doing so. That is why, if our definition of Judaism is taken account of, it is neither appropriate nor accurate to speak of a Judeo-Christian culture or civilisation in relation to the West today. It is enough to call it 'Christian'.

(c) The Church and its portable Land

As Philo of Alexandria, followed by Ireneus[6] and then other Fathers,had asserted, the diaspora person is merely *transient on earth and in his or her own land*; her or his true 'dwelling place', like the one s/he will reach at the end of her or his journey on earth, is in the heavenly kingdom. If s/he can in some way be said to be 'exiled', like the Jew, it is only in relation to his or her final end in life and not in relation to return to some national land. This produces the vast difference there is in the ways the person in diaspora and the person in exile view and manage their relation with the land they live in.

But let us describe in more detail the *relation of Christianity to earth* (not to 'its' earth or 'its' land).

First, it should be remembered that the existence of the Christian as such depends on an objective faith, that is on a Creed and a Church. The limits of both the Church and the Creed are those of the sum of the institutions and practices among which the Bible, as the *canon of the Scriptures*, occupies a special and privileged place. Within the declared framework of the other institutions, Christianity—or rather the Church—puts forward the Bible to read as a 'canon'. Quantitatively, calling it a 'canon' adds nothing to the Bible; it simply means that the Church, which recognises the Bible as its inspired Scriptures, puts it forward to be read everywhere and guarantees the truth of its message. The canonical Bible is therefore the substitute, not of the Temple as the Torah is for the Jews, for in Christianity the Temple exists, and in two different ways, but of the missing one Land. The true Christian homeland, as we have said, is in some sense a heavenly land. How then are we to link that heavenly land with the earthly land every aspect of which is called to become 'Christian'? In this wise: the scriptural canon, like a national Land, has an outline and frontiers. The word canon means 'rule' but also 'measure'. But the canonical matter is open to as many new and different expressions as there are and will be languages on earth. So it can be suggested that, mythically and being as it were almost sacramentally itself, it is a *portable land*. In other words, the canon is the necessary condition for the Bible to take the form of vulgates; in Christianity, the Bible only ever has lived and can only ever live in the guise of a vulgate. In the last analysis this means its canonical quality, the very quality through which the Scriptures are normative and, in their place, a source of faith, is fundamentally constitutive of the Bible.

(*d*) The canonical field and its triple perspective

In the Torah, as we have said and demonstrated, Scripture and Doctrine, and Scripture and Tradition are fused in one and the same whole. In Christianity, as we have already suggested, matters are very different.

The traditional teaching of the Church establishes a dogmatic distinction between Tradition and Scripture, both of which are defined as 'sources of faith'. This duality was reflected in the way we presented the canon of the Scriptures. It was only fairly late, in the fourth century, that the term 'canon' was used of the Bible in a literary sense;[7] previously it had been applied to theological matters in the expression '*canon* of tradition', '*canon* of truth' or 'ecclesiastical *canon*'. This shift in meaning shows clearly the breadth and limits of the use of the word *canon*, 'rule'.

Establishing this 'canonical' field leads us to distinguish between *Christianity* and the *Church*. The canonical field belongs to the Church; it is 'ecclesiastical'. By Church we mean, on the one hand, the hierarchical and worshipping community of the faithful, and, on the other, the apparatus of deposit and management of the objective Faith. By Christianity we mean the more or less world-wide social and doctrinal ensemble which draws its relevance and cohesion from a system of institutions, beliefs, images and practices. The Church, it could be said, is canonical in its essence, and as such is the support or stay, but also the driving force and, above all, the ultimate truth of Christianity. It is the total mediation of the Church that, in Christianity, brings about the integration of the various dimensions that constitute and maintain it;—and with the integration there is necessarily a verificatory tribunal. Beyond the Church and Christianity there is *Christendom*, a political, historical and cultural entity which shapes but also indelibly marks such or such a part of the inhabited world.

This organic view of Christian realities, which are *diaspora realities*, highlights the profound difference between them and Jewish realities, which are *realities of exile*. The triangular or ternary relation Church-Christianity-Christendom has no equivalent and can have no equivalent among the Jews.

CONCLUSION

We are now in a position to answer the questions we formulated at the beginning of this article.

(a) In Christianity, *orthodoxy* emerges primarily as a necessity and not simply as a possibility. It can be said to be inherent in the very system of Christianity: it appears as a private and public force of verification and synthesis, and without it, the constitutive and historically motive articulation Church-Christianity-Christendom would break down. The Christian social-doctrinal system, as we have said, is *centrifugal*, linguistically and culturally as well as geographically and socially. Of itself therefore it needs orthodoxy if it is to survive and be effective.

(b) The situation in Judaism is quite different. The system is *centripetal*. And given what we have said about the function of orthodoxy in Christianity, it immediately appears in Judaism to be neither necessary nor, rigorously speaking, even possible. Its place and function are amply and profoundly compensated for by all the latent forces of the Torah and the system that goes with it. In Judaism, with neither Temple nor hierarchy, orthodoxy is in a sense provided *a priori* by a very strong dose of ideology, that of the 'exile' or 'stranger'. For Christianity revelation is finished, literarily by the closure of the canon, but for Judaism it is still in act. In the last analysis that is the essential basis of the difference.

(c) Since Judaism and Christianity sprang from the same matrix, it is natural, both generally and historically, that there should be sometimes striking similarities between the two systems. In fact for the close observer the similarities merely highlight the difference. They have been maintained by the interplay of mutual overdeterminations which in part conditioned the parallel development of the 'non-identical twins'. It is even possible to hold the view that, though Christianity and Judaism did share a matrix, Judaism would be so different that it would have ceased to exist as a real social-doctrinal system had it not unexpectedly had Christianity as a partner.

Translated by Ruth Murphy

Notes

1. On the distinction between 'Diaspora' and 'Exile' see A. Paul 'Une Voie d'approche du fait juif: Diaspora et Galût, De la Torah au Messie' *Mélanges Henri Cazelles* (Paris 1981) pp. 369–380, and 'La Torah et le canon chrétien: deux suppléances d'un manque politique' *Recherches de Sciences religieuses* 71 (1983) 139–147.

2. As asserted by Philo of Alexandria in *De confusione linguarum* 78.

3. The oldest and most outstanding theory of exile Judaism is in the Greek-language text *The Third Book of Macchabees* (for analysis and commentary in A. Paul 'Le Troisième livre des Macchabées' *Aufstieg und Niedergang der römischen Welt* II.20 (Berlin 1987) pp. 298–335.

4. All the references for the quotations in this section of the article can be found in A. Paul 'La Bible grecque d'Aquila et l'idéologie du iudaïsme ancien' *Aufstieg und Niedergang der römischen Welt* II.20 (Berlin 1987) pp. 221–245.

5. The reader is here referred to several studies by J. Neusner, in particular *Midrash in Context. Exegesis in Formative Judaism. The Foundation of Judaism. Method, Theology, Doctrine.* Part One. *Method* (Philadelphia 1983).

6. See also 1 Peter 1:17.

7. It is no coincidence that the champion of *homoousios* at the Council of Nicea in 325, Athanasius of Alexandria, is also one of the very earliest witnesses to this specific use of the word 'canon'.

James McCue

Bauer's *Rechtgläubigkeit und Ketzerei*

IT IS more than fifty years since Walter Bauer published his epochal *Rechtgläubigkeit und Ketzerei im ältesten Christentum.*[1] Despite its title, the book is really not focused on the problem of orthodoxy and heresy, at least not in the sense that most readers might anticipate. Bauer does not concern himself with the doctrinal content of either orthodoxy or heresy in early Christianity, or with the process or ideas that led some Christians to define certain views as radically incompatible with Christian faith.

The focus of Bauer's interest is quite different. The book is an *attempt to create a new framework within which to rethink the history of early Christianity.* Bauer is concerned with the problem of the relationship of orthodox and heretical bodies of Christians to one another and to their past. In particular, he is concerned to test the traditional view that heresies develop as deviations from an orthodox mainstream. He argues that the traditional view is basically false, that *orthodoxy is simply one of a number of contemporary and coexisting forms of early Christianity.* Orthodoxy would subsequently seem and claims to be the mainstream, but only because it would be the one which finally prevailed.

Bauer used the terms 'orthodoxy' and 'heresy' without intending to imply any normative judgments. It might have suited his purposes better if he had replaced these terms with more neutral ones, but he decided that new terms would simply confuse matters; and so he uses 'orthodoxy' and 'heresy' to refer to the groups who are customarily so labelled. 'Orthodoxy' thus does not mean correct or true doctrine. 'Orthodoxy ... in earliest Christianity' simply refers to that strand of early (second century) Christianity that achieved a position of dominance in the third century and which eventually became the established form of Christianity in the late Roman Empire.

Bauer proposes a basically new approach to the history of early Christianity. He attacks the basic conception of the history of Christianity that is rooted in Acts and is central to Irenaeus and Eusebius, and to most Christian history and self-understanding since. Instead of a Christian mainstream, Bauer attempts to show that in its origins and through the second century Christianity was a *congeries of competing sects*. 'Heresies' went back as directly (or indirectly) to the beginnings of Christianity as did the form of Christianity represented by Ignatius of Antioch or 1 Peter.

Only with the passage of time did 'orthodoxy' come to prevail. Toward the end of the second century it was *the dominant form only in Rome* and in a few other cities influenced by Rome. For the rest, orthodoxy was a minority position among Christians and in many places it was unknown. In such places, Christianity was synonymous with heresy. In many places it was heresy that was the originally implanted form of Christianity; only later was orthodoxy introduced.

Because it was the Roman version of Christianity that eventually prevailed, it was this version that shaped the perspective of those historian-apologists whose works have survived to shape the historical sensibility of subsequent ages. It was this version of Christianity which would determine what writings would survive and what would not. A view of history was eventually established, according to which the mainstream of Christian life was developed around the apostles and their successors, the bishops.

Bauer's book was widely reviewed in Germany at the time of its first appearance, and was more briefly noted elsehwere. *Critical response has been mixed.* Some writers have basically accepted Bauer's thesis, even while expressing some reservation in matters of detail. Others reject the basic thesis, even while finding many of the details suggestive and important. Still others reject it wholesale. Fifty years after the work's first appearace, we are still without a consensus concerning its value.[2]

To assess Bauer's work properly, it is necessary to evaluate separately the *principal positive and negative theses of Bauer's book*; for these vary greatly in value and cogency. His criticism of the received interpretation of early Christian history is much more compelling that the reconstruction which he attempts to put in its place. Even those most favorably disposed to the book will readily agree that Bauer's conclusions often outrun the evidence, and that he overworks the argument from silence; but Bauer's critics have perhaps too quickly concluded that such observations effectively dispose of the book. It will be my argument that Bauer's positive thesis collapses largely under its own weight; but that this does not leave the traditional history in place. Its collapse leaves a vacuum; and the vacuum has not been filled by the historical studies done since the first appearance of the book. Bauer's work leaves us without a serviceable map of the history of earliest Christianity.

Bauer's positive argument is that *practically everywhere except Rome, heresy was the first and dominant form of Christainity*. It was only late in the second century and under Roman influence that orthodoxy was finally able to gain the upper hand. Rome accomplished this by means that were generally somewhat shabby. Buying influence was apparently the most widely used and effective.

This entire argument has been subjected to well-deserved criticism. The argument from silence is everywhere, and again and again Bauer makes the transition from tentatively stated hypothesis to dogmatic affirmation without the intervention of anything that might count as evidence. He pressures texts to make them mean what he is sure that they must mean with a tendentiousness that would make a fundamentalist blush.

Beyond that, much of his argument really does not lead to conclusions as radical as he claims. For example, he devotes the long first chapter to arguing that heterodox Christianity preceded orthodoxy in *Edessa*. He may be correct in this, though much of his argument here seems to me spurious; but even if he is right this would not tell particularly against the Luke–Acts/Irenaeus view of things. On Bauer's own account, Christianity did not come to Edessa until after the time at which, according to Irenaeus, Marcionite and Valentinian forms of Christianity had already broken off from orthodoxy. The traditional view does not require that orthodox priority be achieved in every town. In the fourth century, the Nicene-Athanasian party doubtless conceived of itself as the mainstream from which Arianism deviated and broke off. But this did not lead the orthodox to deny that it was Arian Christianity that first established itself among the nothern tribes. This latter fact was simply irrelevant. Similarly, whether Marcionite or orthodox Christianity was the first to arrive in Edessa in the later second century is simply irrelevant to the larger issue.

In addition, by eschewing in principle any detailed examination of the *content* of the various heretical systems, Bauer overlooked some important counter-evidence. In his study of the *church at Alexandria*, he limited himself simply to identifying the names of prominent early Alexandrian Christians. Until late in the second century these names were all of non-orthodox figures. But by so limiting himself, he overlooked the fact that the Valentinianism known to Clement of Alexandria toward the end of the century was rooted in practically all the major books of the New Testament. Since these were integrated into a working canon only in the third quarter of the century, and so far as we know only in orthodox circles, this suggests a relationship between at least Valentinianism and orthodoxy that is closer to Irenaeus' views than to Bauer's.

Moreover, the very theology of Valentinianism contains reference to the orthodox as the larger body, and thus would also seem to tell against Bauer at least as concerns the Valentinians.[3]

The argument suffers as well from a *rather strange view of the church at Rome* in the first and second centuries. 'Rome', according to Bauer, was already endowed with the expansive and domineering spirit which would characterise it more fully in the age of Gregory VII or Innocent IV. There was a kind of embryonic *Romanità* waiting to emerge. Boniface VIII can almost be discerned waiting in the wings. It is this Roman emphasis which some of the early Catholic reviewers found attractive. Those who doubt such second century anticipations of what was to come will be less impressed. It seems highly questionable whether the Roman church had any conception of itself as having a global mission in the second century. Even Irenaeus' often cited account of the Roman church as a touchstone of orthodoxy does not present Rome as a church that extends itself throughout the world. It is rather a place to which people come from all over the world. The Roman church of the second century had neither the resources, the structure, nor the sense of mission required by Bauer's thesis.

Moreover, it is a bit strange to find Rome characterised as the one church which had never been seriously affected by heresy until well on in the second century. The early Roman church seems not to have been tightly organised. Rome was a centre to which people came from all parts of the empire. That heresy could have been as dominant throughout the Empire in the earlier part of the century, as Bauer would have it, but that Rome would somehow or other have been spared it, seems altogether implausible. But such purity is required by Bauer in order to lend some plausibility to his efforts to make Rome the centre from which orthodoxy extends itself and eventually takes over the Christian world. What was supposedly different about Rome was that it did not have the *internal problems* that plagued so many other churches, and this was one of the factors that made it possible for it to take world-wide leadership in advancing the cause of orthodoxy.

Throughout the book Bauer *argues extensively from silence*. This is always a difficult argument, since one must be able to establish that the silence is significant and not just accidental, that there *ought* to be something there which is missing. An argument from silence, to be persuasive, must present us with an absence that needs explaining and that can only be explained in a particular way. But quite often, Bauer simply uses silence as a space within which to create history out of whole cloth.

These and many other, more detailed, criticisms have been made of Bauer's work. It is a work full of faults. But to focus on the faults is to do the book an injustice. It may well be that Bauer's positive reconstruction of the early history of Christianity collapses under the weight of its own implausibility and *ad hoc* hypotheses; the *de*structive part of his argument remains compelling. Bauer does not know how earliest Christianity developed; but when he is finished neither do we. *His criticism of the received tradition is compelling.*

What is the traditional history? It begins in Luke–Acts with Jesus singling out the apostles as the witnesses par excellence of all that he does both in Galilee and Jerusalem. They witness his death and are repeatedly visited by the risen Jesus, then sent out as the central bearers of the word. Around them the Church coalesces. This motif is elaborated by Irenaeus and the other anti-'gnostic' polemicists of the late second and third centuries. The apostles left behind them the normative apostolic scriptures as well as the apostolic-episcopal ministry, the twin pillars of the Church. The earliest surviving effort to describe the history of the Church from its origins to the present, that of Eusebius of Caesarea, simply orchestrates these themes.

The fact that the bulk of the extant literature fits in with this pattern is not decisive. We have only a very small sampling of what was written in the first three Christian centuries. What we do have is, of necessity, what the surviving and dominant institutions considered it worth while to preserve. How representative this is of what actually existed earlier is a question that cannot be easily answered.

Clearly it was the opinion of Irenaeus and of the other anti-heretical writers that their opponents all represented deviations from the apostolic way established from the beginning. What Bauer makes clear is that their opinion in the matter counts for little. In Bauer's opinion, the heretics of the second century are the descendents of first century varieties of Christianity. Some of them are offshoots of Paul. Others are descended from the opponents of Paul. Still others are descended we know not whence. Earliest Christianity was a congeries of sects, variously related to the originating impulse given by Jesus. There is no reason to suppose that in the beginning there was a single coordinated response to Jesus which only subsequently came apart in several directions. Traditional church history is, in Bauer's view, an apologetic recasting of the story so that the line leads unambiguously from Jesus to the present church establishment. It is religious propaganda.

It may be that Bauer is wrong. It may be that the early history of Christianity was roughly (very roughly) what Irenaeus took it to be. But unfortunately, this could be established, if at all, only by a very different use of sources than has characterised most writing of early Christian history. Irenaeus and Eusebius provide insight into the self-understanding of orthodoxy at important stages along the way. They do not, simply and directly, provide insight into the relationship between orthodoxy and heresy in their own time and earlier. Some resources are available for such study, but they have thus far not been extensively exploited.

What presently seems plausible? Though *Rechtgläubigkeit* is focused on the second century, it has perhaps had its greatest influence among New Testament scholars, especially among Bultmann's students.[4] By posing the question of the relationship of orthodoxy and heresy to the origins of Christianity, Bauer provided a perspective that enabled New Testament scholars to enquire in a new and fruitful way into the *question of plurality in the New Testament* and the relationship of New Testament writers to their opponents. It had always been known that Paul had had adversaries at Corinth and at Colossae, and that the Johannine letters did not represent the views of all Christians within their orbit; but there has been a strong tendency to view these 'others' simply as foils for the canonical writers. They were of interest principally for having provided the canonical writers the opportunity to have their say.

Bauer's proposal, on the other hand, suggests that we think of the New Testament writers *simply as a few voices among the early Christian cacophony*, not as the central or dominating voices. They become 'the New Testament' in virtue of the action of the church of a later time. They stand in no more direct or unmediated a relationship to Jesus the Christ than do their opponents.

This has led to a very un-Lukan picture of New Testament Christianity. *There seems to be no graspable, orginating centre.* Paul's opponents at Corinth or Colossae (supposing that Paul wrote Colossians) came we know not whence. There seems to be no reason to suppose that the originating impulse behind their Christianity was the preaching of the Twelve (or of the Twelve plus Paul). Indeed, Paul's listing, in 1 Corinthians 15, of the various resurrection appearances, would suggest a highly uncoordinated beginning (or set of beginnings) to Christianity. There seems to be no particular reason to suppose that opposition from Paul would have put a stop to the work of the 'pseudoapostles' in Corinth. They seem not to have been much impressed by him earlier, and it would only be much later that he would automatically count as an authority. Consequently, there seems no particular reason to suppose that their type of Christianity could not have had a history down into the second century. Whether or not any plausible connections can be made between these opponents and observable forms of later heresy is another question.

The general scheme, then, of *second century diversity being derivative from first century diversity* rather than being a breaking off from first century unity seems highly plausible. *Two qualifications* must be made, however.

The first is that the evidence is good that *at least some* of the second century heresies were indeed derivative from orthodoxy. I have already suggested that there are indications within Valentinianism itself, and not simply in the polemics against it, that make it reasonably clear that Valentinianism *was* derivative from orthodoxy.

Secondly, the *quantitative* indications are very difficult to assess confidently. Bauer argued that orthodoxy was in the minority almost everywhere but Rome until the end of the second century. Bauer has made clear how problematic is the evidence for great orthodox numerical preponderance. Still, some sources that are independent of the tendencies of Irenaeus and Eusebius seem to reinforce the view that we find in them. The anti-Christian writer Celsus leaves little doubt that 'the great Church' is approximately the one described by Irenaeus. Similarly, Valentinianism seems to presuppose orthodoxy as the mass within which it would be a small leaven. Orthodoxy would thus *seem* to have become the dominant form of Christianity much earlier than Bauer allows. Bauer's thesis could quite possibly be closer to the truth for the first century than for the second, even though the first century is hardly considered in *Rechtgläubigkeit*.

If that is the case, the elaborate explanation of how Rome brought about the triumph of orthodoxy loses its last tenuous link with reality. The triumph would have happened before the church at Rome was in a position to do much of anything.

The *discoveries at Nag Hammadi* have not decisively altered the question for the second century. We now have far more heretical material from the second century than we once had. It now seems clearer that there were forms of Jewish gnosticism that show no evidence of Christian influence. We also now have evidence, if such were needed, that second century forms of Christian gnosticism were not obsessed with their relationship to orthodoxy; that they sometimes quarrelled among themselves. Moreover, some of the New Testament opponents (Colossians, for example) bear a family resemblance to second century gnosticism; but this resemblance is apparent even on the basis of our pre-Nag Hammadi understanding of gnosticism. And the quantitative issue—which form(s) of Christianity dominated where in the second century—is not clarified by the newer documents.

At the time that Bauer published *Rechtgläubigkeit* it could hardly have been given a hearing within Roman Catholicism, except perhaps as evidence that radical Protestant scholarship was coming to recognise an early Roman primacy. The integration of the Acts–Irenaeus version of history into the dogmatic tradition was so substantial that Bauer's thesis would have required profound doctrinal reorganisation. The changes that have taken place within Roman Catholicism since that time would seem to have created the conditions necessary for Bauer to get a careful hearing. It is widely recognised that the traditional history has often been inadequate and self-serving, and that this has had a significant impact on the theological and doctrinal tradition. A major factor in the change in theological consciousness has been a change in historical consciousness. Bauer's work poses in an acute form—because it deals with the very roots of Christian history—the question of the relationship between faith, theological reflection, and history.

Notes

1 Walter Bauer *Rechtgläubigkeit und Ketzerei im ältesten Christentum*, 1934; zweite, durchgeschene Auflage mit einem Nachtrag, hrsg. Georg Strecker, 1964. English translation of the second edition, *Orthodoxy and Heresy in Earliest Christianity*, tr. and ed. by Robert Kraft and Gerhard Krodel, 1971.

2 See 'Die Aufnahme des Buches' *Rechtgläubigkeit* pp. 288–306; ET, pp. 286–316. The English version of this section has been extensively revised by R. Kraft in consultation with G. Strecker.

3 See for example J. McCue 'Orthodoxy and Heresy: Walter Bauer and the Valentinians' *Vigiliae Christianae* 33 (1979) 118–130.

4 See ET, pp. 306–308; the material is not in the German original.

PART II

Systematic Aspects

Anton Houtepen

Hierarchia Veritatum and Orthodoxy

'EVERY RENEWAL of the Church essentially consists in an increase of
fidelity to her own calling. Undoubtedly this explains the dynamism of the
movement towards unity. Christ summons the Church, as she goes her
pilgrim way, to that continual reformation of which she always has need, in
so far as she is an institution of men and women here on earth. Therefore, if
the influence of events or of the times has led to deficiencies in conduct, in
Church discipline or even in the formulation of doctrine (which must be
carefully distinguished from the deposit itself of faith), these should be
appropriately rectified at the proper moment'

(Unitatis Redintegratio § 6)[1]

THE REFORMATION of the Church, which Vatican II had in mind for the
sake of the credibility of faith and the Church's unity and power to recruit
members, is now threatening, after twenty years of changes in the liturgy and
Church order, *to come to a stop.* The liturgical reforms have been more drastic
than the changes in Church order and have proved to be the most fruitful
ecumenically. They have not, however, been sufficient to restore communion
with the churches of the East or the Anglican or Reformed churches, nor have
they been enough to close the gap between doctrine and life in the great
majority of church members. There have been practically no reforms in the
articulation of faith or the guidelines for personal and social behaviour.

Confronted with the factual pluralism of convictions and modes of
behaviour and the description and definition by theologians and religious
sociologists of many key concepts, such as partial identification,
contextuality, freedom of conscience and so on, the Church's teaching
authority seems to want to preserve, in its statements, ways of acting and

39

condemnations, *a pre-conciliar concept of 'orthodoxy'*, in which change in the articulations of faith and the guidelines for human behaviour is tabu. This is not only damaging to the freedom of theology—it is also in contradiction to the logic of the ecumenical dialogue.

The search that takes place in that dialogue is for *new shared criteria for fidelity to faith*, especially via ecumenical theological hermeneutics, in which light is thrown on the relationship between history and Scripture, Scripture and tradition, dogma and the interpretation of the Church's teaching office and finally the text and the context.[2]

The most important insight that we have gained in this ecumenical dialogue, however, is the conviction that the principal function of an articulated confession of faith, the fundamental significance of the New Testament *homologia*, is the *doxology*. The communicative, disciplinary, pedagogical and apologetical functions of this *homologia* are derived from the doxology and are subordinated to it. The concern shown by the Church's *magisterium* for the true *homologia* should therefore be directed less towards the *determinatio fidei*, seen as the precise delineation of the articulations about *fides et mores*, and more towards the *communicatio fidei*, the confession of faith of the believing community, which is able to lead to reciprocal unanimity, a missionary credibility of faith and an authentic encounter with God.[3]

A one-sided emphasis on the *determinatio fidei* leads to rigidity in the articulation of faith. It also tempts theologians to move in the direction of 'grammatology'[4] instead of a direct interpretation of man's search for God and God's saving intentions with people. It therefore makes ecumenical dialogue a specialism of historians of dogma.

It was the intention of Vatican II to prevent this development. In any search for the true *homologia*, a real orthodoxy that creates unity and is communicative, missionary and faithful, the emphasis must be placed on the *material and qualitative content of the Church's confession* and not—or at least not primarily—on the formal and quantitative aspects of that confession. Both in their attempt to reach unity and in their vigilance over fidelity to faith, Church members and their leaders should keep in mind the *rectum ordinem valorum christianorum*, the due order of Christian values. In the light of this right order, they put into practice the reformation called for in the *Decree on Ecumenism* quoted at the beginning of this article. They should, in other words, reform the formulations concerning *fides et mores*.

This seems to be the background to the well-known passage in the same Decree (*Unitatis Redintegratio* § 11) on the *hierarchia veritatum*, the hierarchy of values, the implications of which have hardly been realised since Vatican II. The interpretation of this passage provided by the *magisterium* of the Catholic

Church, which is to be found especially in the Declaration *Mysterium Ecclesiae*, published on 5 February 1973 by the Congregation for the Doctrine of Faith and in a number of papal addresses,[5] on the one hand, and that provided by many Catholic theologians, including recently Charles Curran,[6] on the other, are very different. For this reason, a rereading of the original intentions is urgently required and this should be carried out both with the progress of ecumenical dialogue in mind and in order to overcome internal polarisation. The final and perhaps most important aim in this rereading is to strengthen the missionary credibility of faith of the Church in every kind of context. The last two aspects are discussed in detail elsewhere in this number. I shall therefore confine myself in this article to the significance of *Unitatis Redintegratio* § 11 for ecumenical dialogue, even though it may emerge that this has certain consequences for our understanding of 'orthodoxy' as such.

1. HIERARCHIA VERITATEM DOCTRINAE CATHOLICAE:

From *integra doctrina* to *investigabiles divitiae Christi* (Eph 3:8)

The manner and order in which Catholic belief is expressed should in no way become an obstacle to dialogue with our brethren. It is, of course, essential that doctrine be clearly presented in its entirety *(integra doctrina)* ... At the same time, Catholic belief needs to be explained more profoundly and precisely, in ways which our separated brethren too can really understand. Furthermore, Catholic theologians engaged in ecumenical dialogue, while standing fast by the teaching of the Church and searching together with separated brethren into the divine mysteries, should act with love for truth, with charity and with humility. When comparing doctrines, they should remember that in Catholic teaching there exists *an order or 'hierarchy' of truths, since they vary in their relationship to the foundation of the Christian faith.* Thus the way will be opened for this kind of fraternal rivalry to incite all to a deeper realisation and a clearer expression of the *unfathomable riches of Christ* (cf. Eph 3:8).

(Unitatis Redintegratio § 11)[7]

The above text has often been discussed and various authors have called it the most revolutionary and prophetic pronouncement made by Vatican II.[8] The history of both its development and its effectiveness, which has recently been subjected to a detailed reanalysis by H. Witte,[9] show clearly that *it has to be interpreted against the background of the Catholic understanding of dogma that had prevailed since Vatican I.* It should also more particularly be read as a reaction to and a subtle qualification of the passage from the Constitution on Faith, *Dei Filius*, § 3 of Vatican I, which provided a formal and quantitative definition of the Catholic concept of 'orthodoxy':

> Therefore, with divine and Catholic faith, all must be believed that is contained in the written and transmitted Word of God and has been put forward by the Church by a solemn pronouncement or by the ordinary and universal teaching authority as revealed from God to be believed'.[10]

This passage was clearly directed against nineteenth century developments which aimed to introduce differentiations into the validity of doctrinal statements made by the Church by limiting the obligatory content of faith to the confession solemnly formulated by the Church's councils or *ex cathedra* by the bishop of Rome. The passage quoted above is a direct rejection of the positions taken at the congress of theologians held at Munich in 1863 under the leadership of von Döllinger.[11]

It was, then, right that Vatican I should be opposed to a *minimalism of dogma*, which suggested that the normative confession and therefore the orthodoxy of the Church coincided with the Church's solemn definitions and that preaching and liturgy, theology and episcopal letters were no more than a non-obligatory commentary alongside a juridically firmly established but minimal deposit of faith. This minimalism, however, changed after Vatican I and especially during the Church's conflict with Modernism into a typically Roman Catholic *maximalism of dogma*, which claimed that every magisterial pronouncement and every encyclical letter or *breve* had the character of a revelation.

Every distinction between fundamental and non-fundamental articles of faith—a traditional theological distinction which had been developed in the Reformation and in the Anglican tradition and which had long proved useful in ecumenical dialogue—was rejected by Pius XI in his Encyclical *Mortalium Animos*.[12] No Catholic doctrinal statements could ever be discussed, let alone abandoned, in ecumenical dialogue. This integralism and immobility, which predominated until 1950 and is even discernible in the Encyclical *Humani Generis* of that year,[13] made participation by Catholics in any true ecumenical dialogue impossible. It brought about a fundamental 'ecclesiological asymmetry' and made theologians into mere 'scribes of the Church's *magisterium*'. It was the theological motivation underlying the Catholic model of unity. Yves Congar has called it a 'conception of unity of a uniform and hierarchised military type'.[14]

There was, of course, the system of 'theological qualifications'.[15] This accepted *gradations in the obligatory character of the formulations of faith*, not only according to their place within the *hierarchia auctoritatum* (in which the words of Scripture enjoyed a higher authority than the pronouncements of individual Church Fathers, bishops or theologians), but also according to their direct or less direct relationship to the 'revealed truth', even when solemn statements concerning faith were concerned.

This system had been developed in scholasticism as a means of distinguishing between *genera veritatum catholicarum*[16] and had been extended in the fourteenth and fifteenth centuries, when it became a more or less generally accepted *hierarchia auctoritatum*.[17] This hierarchy of *authorities* was also taken over by the Reformation and refined in the theological genre of *loci theologici* in the work of Melchior Cano and Melanchthon, who developed it into a method of argument.

In many respects, it provided a counterbalance to the prevailing 'discipline of doctrine', which was far too strict. It was therefore possible for L. Choupin to point out in 1907—at the height of the conflict with Modernism—that even 'infallible' pronouncements made by the bishop of Rome, that is, definitive decisions regarding *fides et mores* which were made *ex cathedra*, did not have by definition to be accepted *de fide* if they were related to dogmatic questions further along the line of deduction. Non-acceptance of such doctrinal statements could therefore not be regarded as 'heresy' (*haeresis*).[18]

G. Thils has pointed out that not everything that is handed on to Catholics by the Church's teaching authority as an orientation for faith and life automatically has validity for *all Christians*. Statements which were made by leaders of the Catholic Church during the period following the great divisions that took place in 1054 and 1517 can therefore hardly claim the same universal validity as the statements made by the *first seven or eight ecumenical councils*.[19]

In the dialogue with Anglicans, there has been an investigation into the possibility of not making the last three solemn Roman Catholic dogmatic statements (1854, 1870 and 1950) the condition for the restoration of *communio*, on the basis both of their narrower universal authority and of their remote connection with direct revelation.[20] In the dialogue with the non-Chalcedonian churches, the Secretariat for Unity has even called for the acceptance of the formulations of Chalcedon not to be made a condition *sine qua non* for the restoration of *communio*.[21]

Merely on the basis of the differentiations that have already been made in the question of the formal validity of dogmatic formulations, there is scope, then, for dialogue and, *mutatis mutandis*, also for a pluralism of formulations within the same Catholic *communio* of churches. The fact that the Uniate Catholics of the Eastern rite are allowed to use the Nicaean-Constantinopolitan Creed without the addition of the *Filioque* clause is a striking example of this scope.

There is, however, a very real danger that this path may take us in the direction of an *oppressive casuistry of dogma*, which in addition has a rather anachronistic flavour in the presence of the many recent critical questions surrounding the classical confession and Christian behaviour that are constantly arising in all the churches today. It is good, then, that, bearing in mind the history of the development of *Unitatis Redintegratio* § 11, there is, apart from a reference to these *genera veritatum catholicarum* and, with it, a reference to formal criteria for the validity of the Church's pronouncements, also a *reference to the 'foundation of the Christian faith' as the criterion of dogma that has a far more qualitative content.*

The text quoted above from *Unitatis Redintegratio* § 11 goes back directly to an amendment made by the Brazilian Bishop Ferraz, who was himself a convert from Protestantism. It was, moreover, made within the framework of the question regarding the *need to recognise the positive values of the Reformation* and to approach the Anglican churches positively and to reassess the question of their ordinations. According to Bishop Ferraz, schisms were the historical consequence of placing a too exclusive emphasis on certain dogmas which had at the time become neglected, but concerning which there was a consensus of opinion. Examples of this were such questions as justification on the basis of faith and works, the concept of original sin, conversion and sanctification and the value of the scriptures.[22]

An intervention by Cardinal Léger of Montreal, who criticised *dogmatic immobility*, also lies in the background of this text. We are indebted to him for the reference to the 'unfathomable riches of Christ' (Eph 3:8), which places the search for truth in a missionary and eschatological context. *Integra fides*—orthodoxy—always remains a provisional task. That is why Catholics also have to *'search together' with others* for the meaning of God's mysteries.[23]

Dom Hoeck reminded the Council in his intervention that, as the canon of the articulation of faith, dogma is always the dogma of a *concrete community of faith* and that this also applies to the scriptures. In that sense, apart from the common centre, Christ, 'fundamental articles of faith' are understood differently by the Reformation from how they are understood by the Church of Rome or the Orthodox churches. Seen in this light, what can be accepted by *all Christians* is given a higher priority. In the ecumenical dialogue itself, then, a new *'hierarchy of truths' gradually emerges* through a concentration on the central mystery of Christ, by the establishment of a consensus and various convergences and by a distinction being made between matters of primary and matters of secondary importance.[24]

O. Cullmann and W. Visser 't Hooft saw in this final point the real and even the revolutionary significance of *Unitatis Redintegratio* § 11.[25] All the churches had the task of carrying out this plan of concentration and of openly discussing their own *hierarchia veritatum*.

This, however, did not succeed in making it quite clear *which* concrete order was meant here within *Catholic* dogma, nor was it obvious how the 'foundation of the Christian faith' could be defined.

Archbishop Pangrazio of Gorizia made an intervention in which he distinguished between the essential aspects of the mystery of Christ belonging to the order of the *end* (such as the Trinity, the Incarnation, the Redemption, grace, eternal life and the Kingdom of God) and those aspects forming part of the order of the *means* of salvation (such as the seven sacraments, the hierarchical structure of the Church, the apostolic succession, the primacy of the bishop of Rome and so on). Pangrazio insisted that the second were subordinate to the first and that the divided nature of Christianity was based less on the order of the end and much more on the order of the means of salvation. What he seemed to be indicating was that this was bound to set dialogue free from its restrictions and let the unity that was already present play a much more important part.[26]

Pangrazio's distinction corresponded to Thomas Aquinas' distinction between *credibilia secundum se* and *credibilia in ordine ad alia*, but he gave it an entirely different content. Thomas' *credibilia secundum se* coincide with the articles of faith, that is, the Apostles' Creed, and his *credibilia in ordine ad alia* were identical with what later came to be known as *facta dogmatica*: the details of the history of salvation, in other words, that Abraham had two sons and so on.[27]

Pangrazio's distinction was, however, not accepted by the Council and no attempt was made to define the order. There was a feeling that the question concerning the precise formulation of the 'foundation of the Christian faith' should be left open. It was in any case not the Church itself or the *magisterium*, nor was it formulated dogma, Scripture, the Creed or anything like the basis of the World Council of Churches or any other 'abbreviated formulae of faith'. The foundation of faith is the mystery of God and of Christ himself.[28]

There was clearly some hesitation about choosing between a *more theocentric and a more Christocentric approach*.[29] The same hesitation or preference can also be found in the work of those theologians who tried to interpret the Decree *Unitatis Redintegratio* in greater detail after the Council. It is important to point out that *a Christocentric confession leads to a Trinitarian doxology*, whether this is seen in a historical perspective in the development of the conciliar dogma during the fourth and fifth centuries or whether it is considered in the more recent discussions about the basis of the World Council of Churches[30] and the structure of a great number of contemporary confessions of faith.[31] In the dialogue with Israel and the non-Christian religions, however, what is required is a primarily theocentric approach to the foundation of the confession and the *hierarchia veritatum*.

Vatican II has made both approaches possible. This is clear from the Constitution on the Church, *Lumen Gentium* § 1 and §§ 13–15.

What, then, can we learn from this history of the development of this text in the Decree on Ecumenism? We may conclude that, both for the ecumenical dialogue and for the establishment of internal criteria for fidelity to faith, the mystery of Christ is the 'foundation of the Christian faith'. Or rather, Jesus himself, confessed as the Christ, the Kurios of his Church, is the centre of the homology that unifies everyone. Within that homology, which requires articulations with the *communicatio fidei* in mind, there is a hierarchy of truths which have to be 'weighed' against each other and in dialogue with each other and not simply summarised as a list of important and less important dogmatic 'obligations'.

In this, the word *veritates* does not merely refer to the noetic component of the confession, but, according to the history of the development of the text, it also has the meaning of an *ordo valorum christianorum*, an order of Christian *values*, and therefore also includes ecclesial elements and aspects of the praxis of faith that cannot be separated from the confession. If confession, celebration and service, if bearing witness, liturgy and the praxis of Christian living together form the pillars of the Christian *koinonia*, then it must be possible for all three to be the subject of more central or more inferential articulation. In the ecumenical dialogue, all three have to be 'weighed' and the insights of the partners in the dialogue have to be verified and, via their 'concentration' on the centre of the homology, brought into unity with each other. A similar concentration is also intended in the case of *ethics*. It would therefore be wrong to regard all ethical values as having a lower priority in the *hierarchia veritatum*, as Curran would seem to indicate. It would, however, be even more wrong to exclude all discussion about ethics from the ecumenical dialogue and from the Church generally.

By a 're-reception' of their own tradition and in dialogue with other church traditions and with the different movements and modalities within their own circle, the churches must formulate new 'convergences' that will make it possible to concentrate on what is most essential. That is, as can be seen from the developments concerned with the Faith and Order report, very different from a search for the greatest common factor or the lowest common multiple (which was called a 'false irenicism' in *Unitatis Redintegratio* § 11). It is rather—and this is what the text has in mind—a search for a new, shared articulation of the one *fides catholica*.[32] I will attempt in the section that follows to enlarge on this question.

2. HIERARCHIA VERITATUM

as the Hermeneutical Principle for the Ecumenical Dialogue

Together with the Constitution on the Church, *Lumen Gentium* § 8 and §§ 13–15, and the Decree on the Church's Missionary Activity, *Ad Gentes*, *Unitatis Redintegratio* § 11 has, with its reference to the *hierarchia veritatum*, pointed to a *change in the Catholic Church's understanding of itself as the exclusive figure and protector of evangelical truth*. But has the abandonment of the claim that it is the only true Church of Christ also really led to such radical reforms that the partners in the ecumenical dialogue are able to see their own concentration on what is essential reflected also in the *Catholica*, with the result that it has gradually become possible to speak authentically of a new and ecumenical orthodoxy?

Multilateral and bilateral dialogue has been taking place for twenty years now and the answer to that question is still far from clear. So far, the various forms of dialogue have only taken place at the level of the 'order of the means'. To go back to Pangrazio's point, discussion has been about the sacraments, the Church's offices, the *magisterium* and models of unity. It is only in the multilateral dialogue of Faith and Order that the participants have concentrated on an *ecumenical confession of faith*, even though this has so far only been by concentrating on the historical text of the Niceno-Constantinopolitan Creed.[33]

Does this mean that we are in agreement about the 'order of the end' or does it rather mean that we have begun on the wrong side in the *hierarchia veritatum* and that we have not yet spoken about our really fundamental differences?[34]

Although many would claim that the second explanation is correct, I believe that a third conclusion is more realistic. The distinction made by Pangrazio is, in my opinion, illusory. It is defective because it is *based on a wrong view of the Church and of salvation*. There is, after all, only one ecumenical task and that is to bring the churches together and to bring about a reconciliation between people within that process. People have to be reconciled with their traditions of confession, their liturgical forms and their ethical and organisational choices. This mutual reconciliation has, moreover, to take place within one *koinonia* of free, very diverse groups, movements and local churches with their many contextual overtones.

There is no *ecumene*, above or outside the churches, of theological agreements about the Trinity, the Incarnation, grace or eternal life. The Church—the *ekklesia tou theou*—is, after all, itself the figure of salvation and both the way and the end, at least in so far as the historical order is concerned. There is a temptation which is not entirely remote from the distinction made by the Reformation between fundamental and non-fundamental articles and which is also a dominant undercurrent in the Lima text.[35] That is to regard the Church as having a lower rank in the order of salvation. This view, however, is detrimental to God's concrete *oikonomia* and all too easily makes man's response in faith degenerate into an abstract gnosis about 'God in himself', relationships within the Trinity, the mystery of the Incarnation and eternal life. This leads to an ontology of nature and grace or of sin and grace, in which the living person and the repentant sinner disappear from sight as believers who are joined together by God in the Church. Neither God nor his salvation can be discussed outside the symbolic *universum* of believers and outside the structures of the faith that we have inherited from Israel and that bind Jesus to his own, even though God's salvation cannot be identified either with Israel or with the Church or located anywhere within them.

With H. Mühlen[36]—and also with all the Church Fathers since Ignatius of Antioch, especially Irenaeus and Augustine, and with Thomas Aquinas—we have therefore not only to include the Church and the sacraments within the framework of the highest truths and values of faith, but also *make the Church character of all thinking, speaking and acting in faith the highest truth and value of faith within the ecumenical dialogue*. A relationship with the mystery of Christ, the centre and the foundation of the identity of the Jesus movement, cannot be obtained separately. That relationship is constitutive for the Church and the reverse is also true. There are therefore no truths of faith that are separate from the faith of belivers. There is—to quote Thomas Aquinas once more—no *perceptio divinae veritatis tendens in ipsam*, perception of divine truth tending towards him, that is separate from the concrete confession of the believers who confess. The whole language of faith—both in the form of dogma and in the form of praise and even as theological *doctrina*—and also all indications regarding moral behaviour—both in the form of 'commandments' and in the form of Church discipline and even in the form of moral theology or Christian ethics—are therefore instruments of the life of faith led by disciples, followers of Jesus, people who say 'amen' to God's *'emunah* and are therefore effective in history only by acting from God.

It is, of course, true that the theological tradition has provided us with a treatise on ecclesiology that has given *an absolute value to the Church*, the sacraments and the Church's offices as means to the end. This is as though God's salvation is only to be found in them and as though God can only be located in holy temples, rites and leaders. The Reformation was the prophetic protest made against this temple ideology and its defenders in the East and the West. It is, however, precisely for this reason that the part played by the community of faith in God's conduct of affairs with people should be the point of departure for the ecumenical dialogue. This is also precisely what Vatican II wanted to do and it is difficult to accept that such a soteriological concentration on the Church as the 'people of God' should be regarded as being so insignificant within the *hierarchia veritatum*.

Very many concrete questions are arising now concerning the place of the sacraments in the life of believers, the relationship between Church leaders and members of the Church, the calling of women to the service of the Word and the sacrament, the relationship between the local and the universal Church and the need for practical political commitment to peace and justice and to social and economic solidarity with the poor. These problems cannot be solved without a radical discussion about the nature of God's *oikonomia* and the meaning of the mystery of Christ. But such a discussion will therefore inevitably lead to doctrinal reforms and to the formulation of common criteria for the *communicatio fidei*, which is necessary for the advancement of a true orthodoxy and orthopraxis.

Seen against the background of the intentions of Vatican II as a whole, the central significance of *Unitatis Redintegratio* § 11, then, would seem to be that the *confessing churches should take each others' listening tradition seriously*. They should all accept the mystery of Christ as the foundation, but they should also give prominence to various emphases in it applicable to faith in God's threefold *oikonomia*, to the relationship between God and man and between history and the Kingdom of God and to the form of the *koinonia* of the Church.

Because everyone's contextual perspective is limited and no one can bear in mind every aspect of the Christian tradition simultaneously, there can never be one single unique *aggiornamento*, after which everything can remain as it always has been. *Aggiornamento* will always be a permanent task. This can be made clearer by a concrete example. The statements made in the Constitution of the First Vatican Council, *Pastor Aeternus*, which, even with the amplifications provided by Vatican II, has proved to be an insurmountable obstacle to ecumenical dialogue with both the Eastern and the Western churches, must be once more debated in the spirit of *Unitatis Redintegratio* § 11 and this debate must take place between sister churches, *pari cum paro* (*Unitatis Redintegratio* § 9).

This is not because these statements are less important in the *hierarchia veritatum*—the members of ARCIC have stressed this and their statement has been contradicted by Cardinal Josef Ratzinger—but because the partners in the ecumenical dialogue have so far been *insufficiently aware in this question of its relationship with the central mystery of Christ*. It is no longer acceptable simply to see in it a 'hardness of heart', a conscious *haeresis*, a defective conception of the Church or an anti-Roman feeling.

The anti-Gallicanistic perspective of *Pastor Aeternus* makes this

Constitution above all a pronouncement about the relationship between the primatial and the conciliar *magisterium*. The question regarding the relationship with the source of this way of speaking (Scripture and Tradition) was discussed in the council's debates, but it is not found in the definition of the dogma itself. The same applies to the question of the place of the reception by believers as a whole of the articulation of faith (*infallibilitas in credendo* and the *sensus fidei fidelium*). It also certainly applies to the question of the eschatological direction of the biblical *matheteuein*: the extent to which magisterial statements are directed towards the criteria of the Kingdom of God.

What is lacking in the definition of Vatican I, then, is the fundamental principle that was included by Vatican II in *Unitatis Redintegratio* § 11—*the relationship to the central mystery of Christ*, understood as the content of the *paradosis* which is directed towards the Kingdom of God. The churches that have rejected Vatican I on this point are therefore not arbitrarily or heretically rejecting a part of that *paradosis*, as was for a long time suggested by the Catholic Church. On the contrary, what they cannot accept is the paradosis character of this statement. No further light was thrown on this problem even by Vatican II.

Is it, then, not heterodox to make such a dogmatic pronouncement the point of dialogue and the commitment to a new formulation? According to *Unitatis Redintegratio* § 11, it certainly is not. Anyone taking part in the ecumenical dialogue and holding out the hand of *koinonia* with a deeper penetration into the truth and a better approach to the 'foundation of the Christian faith' in mind ends—at least *in voto*—the *haeresis* that exists in selecting on the basis of one's own authority and giving an absolute value to statements formulated by earlier councils in opposition to the deliberation of present and the future councils or to decisions taken by partial councils in opposition to those taken by truly universal and ecumenical councils.

Participation in the ecumenical dialogue has the character at least of a *pre-conciliar deliberation*. Readiness to take part in that dialogue in a search for the 'unfathomable riches of Christ' is par excellence the present norm of 'orthodoxy'. Authentic heresy is refusing to hold out the hand of *koinonia*. This is a lesson made clear to us by what the presbyter, John, said about Diotrephes, 'who likes to put himself first and does not acknowledge my authority ... who refuses to welcome the brethren and also stops those who want to welcome them and puts them out of the church' (3 John 9–10).

Translated by David Smith

Notes

1. 'Decree on Ecumenism' *The Documents of Vatican II* (London 1972) p. 350.

2. See the studies of the teaching authority of Faith and Order in 1976 and 1977: 'How Does the Church Teach Authoritatively Today?' in *Verbindliches Lehren der Kirche heute (Beiheft zur Oekumenischen Rundschau* 33, Frankfurt 1978); see *The Bible. Its Authority and Interpretation in the Ecumenical Movement* (Faith and Order Paper 99) eds. E. Flesseman and van Leer (Geneva 1980), and the two ARCIC reports, 'Authority in the Church' I and II in *Growth in Agreement* eds. H. Meyer and L. Vischer (New York and Geneva 1984) pp. 88–118.

3. See A. Houtepen 'Bekenntnisse der Kirchen—Bekenntnis der Oekumene' *Una Sancta* 40 (1985) 62–81; E. Schlink *Oekumenische Dogmatik* pp. 33–67.

4. Claude Geffré *Le Christianisme au risque de l'interprétation* (Paris 1983).

5. *AAS* 65 (1973) pp. 396–408. See also John Paul II's letter to the West German bishops: *AAS* 72 (1980) pp. 385–393.

6. *Origins* 15 (1986) No. 47 p. 771.

7. 'Decree on Ecumenism' cited in note 1, p. 354.

8. O. Cullmann 'Comments on the Decree on Ecumenism' *ER* 17 (1965) 63; see also J. Tillard 'Oecumenisme et Eglise catholique' *NRTh* 107 (1985) 55–56.

9. H. Witte 'Alnaargelang hun band met het fundament van het christelijke geloof verschillend is' in *Wording en verwerking van de uitspraak over de 'hierarchie' van waarheden van Vaticanum II* (Tilburg 1986). Witte's study is an essential amplification of U. Valeske's work *Hierarchia Veritatum* (Munich 1968).

10. DS 3011.

11. DS 2879 and Mansi 53, 192C; 51, 47C.224–225.

12. DS 3683.

13. DS 3884–3885.

14. Y. Congar *Diversités et Communion* (Paris 1982) p. 65.

15. P. Fransen 'Enkele opmerkingen over de theologische kwalificaties' *Hermeneutics of the Councils and Other Studies* (Louvain 1985) pp. 361–381.

16. Y. Congar *La Tradition et les traditions* (Paris 1960) p. 128ff.

17. A. Lang *Die theologischen Prinzipien der mittelalterlichen Scholastik* (Freiburg Basle and Vienna 1964) p. 112ff.; *ibid. Die loci theologici des Melchior Cano und die Methode des dogmatischen Beweises* (Munich 1925).

18. L. Choupin *Valeur des décisions doctrinales et disciplinaires du Saint Siège* (Paris 1907) p. 22.

19. G. Thils *L'Infaillibilité pontificale* (Gembloux 1969) pp. 158–162. This idea was also initially defended by Cardinal Ratzinger in *Theologische Prinzipienlehre* (Munich 1982) pp. 209–211. His text was written in 1976, but was later included in his reaction to the ARCIC Final Report; see J. Ratzinger 'Probleme und Hoffnungen des anglikanisch-katholischen Dialogs' *Internationale katholische Zeitschrift Communio* 12 (1983) 244–259, especially 254–255.

20. ARCIC, Authority I No. 24 and II No. 30, *Growth in Agreement*, cited in note 2, pp. 98 and 114.

21. Information Service SPCU (1974) No. 24 pp. 14–17; see also P. Gregorios *et*

al. Does Chalcedon Divide or Unite? Towards Convergence in Orthodox Christology (Geneva 1981) pp. 1–16.

22. H. Witte, the article cited in note 9, p. 31ff.

23. *Ibid.* p. 42ff.; see also Christian Duquoc *Des Eglises provisoires* (Paris 1985) pp. 97–115.

24. H. Witte, the article cited in note 9, p. 75ff.

25. W. Hryniewicz 'La Hiérarchie des vérités. Implications oecuméniques d'une idée chrétienne' *Irén* 51 (1978) 470–491; see also U. Valeske, the work cited in note 9, pp. 49–52.

26. H. Witte, the article cited in note 9, 45ff.; U. Valeske, the work also cited in note 9, p. 26.

27. *ST* 2a–2ae. q. 1 a. 6 ad 1; see also U. Valeske, the work cited in note 9, pp. 71–77.

28. H. Witte, the article cited in note 9, 290ff.

29. *Ibid.* 162ff., especially 179.

30. *Ibid.* 162ff., especially 179.

31. P. Hoogeveen 'Belijden' *Context* I and II (Utrecht 1985); see also *Confessing our Faith around the World* I–V ed. H. Schlink (Geneva 1983–1986).

32. See M. Thurian *et al. Ecumenical Perspectives on Baptism, Eucharist and Ministry* (Faith and Order Paper 116) (Geneva 1983).

33. See the themes in *Growth in Agreement.* For the Faith and Order study, see *Apostolic Faith Today. A Handbook for Study* (Faith and Order Paper 124) ed. H. G. Link (Geneva 1985).

34. H. Meyer 'Fundamental Difference—Fundamental Consensus' *Midstream* 25 (1986) 247–259.

35. *Churches Respond to Baptism, Eucharist and Ministry* I and II (Faith and Order Papers 129 and 132) ed. M. Thurian (Geneva 1986).

36. H. Mühlen 'Die Bedeutung der Differenz zwischen Zentraldogmen und Randdogmen fur den okumenischen Dialog' in *Freiheit in der Begegnung* eds. J. L. Leuba and H. Stirnmann (Frankfurt and Stuttgart 1969) pp. 191–227.

Alphonse Ngindu Mushete

The Notion of Truth in African Theology

1. A THEOLOGY FOR AFRICA

JOHN XXIII had said: 'The Church in Africa will be African or nothing.'[1]
The African cardinal, B. Gantin, glossed this as follows: '*Theology in Africa will be African or nothing*. This means that it will be Africans' own work, deploying the categories of their culture and informed by their sensibility and their own genius, although it will be as limited as any human enterprise inevitably is.'[2]

Those who keep up with the theological scene and dialogue in Africa know that over the past ten years African theology has been not merely a programme but a living and specifiable reality. 'African theology exists', notes Fr Maurier. 'It's easily found. Let's not talk about "working" theology, the theology taught in seminaries, employed in meetings, retreats, sermons, the theology used by the basic communities, pastors and bishops in conference. Let's talk just about what can be exported in writing ... and what comes out as reflective and systematic work. There is a great deal of this sort of theology around.'[3]

Quite apart from its intrinsic value, the movement of African theology represents a *cultural and ecclesial phenomenon of considerable importance today*.

Several recent works,[4] numerous articles in reviews, a set of themes, ideas and formulae are gripping more and more people and express a movement that is growing. Pastors and theologians, priests and layfolk, religious sisters and brothers are being drawn into something like a ground-swell. As Malcon M. Veigh writes: 'African theology is very much alive and active. It is at a time

53

of excitement and ferment. The new is emerging, ideas and perspectives that will enrich not only Africa and the African Church but world Christianity. The Church universal will do well to follow the debate.'[5]

Since the setting up in 1977 of the Ecumenical Association of African Theologians (AOTA) there has been intense theological activity, ecumenical, inter-university and highly scientific, in both senses of that term: positive and speculative.[6]

As in all such cases, the unity of thought allows of differences of emphasis, even notable divergences. Thus Mgr Tshibangu has a greater concern for balance than Eboussi, who is more cutting, sometimes even brutal, and who speaks as if an alienated belief were on trial. Eboussi writes in particular: '*When we ask whether the African or an African, aware of who s/he is and what continuities and solidarities s/he has, can be Christian, we are interrogating ourselves about the original sense of Christianity, up stream from dogmas, or nearer the source.*'[7]

I must, however, add an observation: African theology has not just emerged by spontaneous generation. It is one of the consequences of the movements of liberation and conquest of political and cultural autonomy that have marked the history of the Black continent so deeply for thirty years now. To be more precise, I must mention the movement for 'Negritude' and the decisive work of the Société Africaine de Culture and particularly its founder, Alioune Diop.

At the level of strictly theological reflection, we should also note the *influence of Vatican II* and its teaching on the collegiality, co-responsibility and communion that should prevail between the old and the young churches. It seems to me that we are not sufficiently aware of the fact that the ideas of co-responsibility and ecclesial communion are so central, decisive and fertile that they alone already contain within themselves a whole theology of the local church. And we can add the emergence, *right across the ecumenical movement*, of similar preoccupations in the heart of the World Council of Churches. In May 1974 the third assembly of the Pan-African Conference of Churches (CETA), which met in Lusaka, challenged the young churches of Africa to ask for a *moratorium on overseas aid*, whether of people or of money. The main point of the debate triggered off in all the churches by the moratorium is obviously the urgent necessity to throw off the paralysing fetters of their dependence on foreign aid and to find, on the spot, ways and means of becoming autonomous and responsible ecclesial communities. The great merit of CETA's appeal for a moratorium lies in its not having rested content with declarations of intent and in having formulated precisely a programme of actions to shake off the tutelage of their sister-churches in the West.

The objective analysis of the situation of the African peoples, in Africa as well as in the diaspora, shows that the domination that came in with *colonialism* still weighs on them. This oppression takes various forms today: racism in South Africa, neo-colonialism pretty well everywhere, under-development exacerbated by the economic exploitation of the great powers, cultural imperialism disguised by a thousand inoffensive names.

This state of affairs persists within the churches: the *model imported from the West is still imposed and accepted* and the local churches are kept in a state of minority spiritually and institutionally as well as materially. It also obtains in theological reflection. The doctrines worked out by the missionary schools and going by such names as theology of the conversion of the pagans, stepping stones, the implantation of the Church have suffused and still largely suffuse the life of the African churches.

Despite the efforts to open things up made by Vatican II and by the World Council of Churches, it is the Western models conveyed by a methodology, a certain way of reading the Bible and a conception of what it is to be a human being specific to the West that continue to prevail.

It is not out of masochism or for the pleasure of inducing guilt-feelings that it remains important to recall this history. It is out of a concern for truth. It is in order to find out whether this process has finished. Finally it is in order to check whether we have understood that all evangelisation involves the *translation of the message to be transmitted,* that is, its presentation in such a way that its meaning can be taken in, assimilated by those to whom it is addressed, can be interpreted by them in the working out of their own theology and for the building up of their church. This is the pre-condition of an evangelisation being meaningful, that is to say, being a factor in development, cultural reactivation, animation and sensitisation—in a word, of salvation.

Within the Church this movement to give peoples back their identities and their liberty so that they rediscover themselves as peoples and refind themselves in their distinctness, needs first of all to be recognised. It presupposes justice being done to the will of the peoples to build themselves up as a society in the way they want to and to construct their church according to their own genius. What is at stake here is the *whole problem of the local churches.*[8] But for this to be at stake in a really concrete fashion the church in Europe needs to begin by asking *forgiveness* of all the peoples it has evangelised, asking pardon for certain narrownesses of view, for certain displays of eurocentric triumphalism and certain contaminations by secular interests.

These facts are well known. And it has become banal and even tedious to recall them. But it is important to underline this here: it is in this context of preoccupations that we have to situate and understand the theology we are being presented with.

2. THE THREE CHARACTERISTICS OF AFRICAN THEOLOGY

African theology has been marked by three characteristics since 1970. It firmly maintains the link between religion and culture; it is very sensitive to the problems of the world and development; it is ecumenical and open to relations with different religions in the world.

(a) A Theology of Culture

African theologians are in the process of turning the missionary theories about the salvation of infidels and adaptation inside out by working out a resolutely *inductive theology of non-Christian religions*. One overriding conviction presides over their procedure, and this is that one can speak validly about the sense of God in another culture only if one is oneself anchored in one's own. We think of ourselves today as *situated beings*—sociologically and historically. In fact we can have the experience of meeting another religion only via tradition understood as a language. Hermeneutics thus becomes *dialogue* to the extent that one remains grounded in one's own tradition and acknowledges that one's understanding is historical.

This has been very well seen and analysed by the Zairean theologian, O. Bimwenyi. The revelation that comes from God (the theic pole) is addressed to human beings who are historically and culturally conditioned (the andric pole). Two fundamental poles of the process of revelation in so far as it is a process of communication. Two essential and constitutive poles which cannot swallow each other up without cancelling out the reality of the message and compromising the communication.[9]

This is the theandric structure of the experience of faith: *Christian religious language emerges and takes on sense only in the heart of a pre-existent religious language, which it assumes, fulfills and transfigures.* What this means concretely is that the human and religious experience of the peoples of Africa constitutes the privileged locus for the meeting with and recognition of Christ on the part of Africans.

In this light one begins to see that the basic question for us is not simply: How are we to make Christ African? but rather: How are we to understand, confess and think Christ present in the heart of our African history and cultures?

This theology has a direct relevance to the Christian mission in Africa today. *It can no longer start from the universality of Christianity as that used to be affirmed abstractly and dogmatically, it must start from its particularity.* The abstract consideration of Christianity as a universal religion easily leads to imperialism. Contrariwise, Christianity considered as one religion among others forces us to think of God not as some *a priori* inscribed in one tradition alone, exclusive, intolerant and conquering, but as a mystery, an eschatological problem of the meeting of cultures in their insurmountable diversity. We meet God in the meetings he provokes. And his face will be unveiled fully only on the last day. 'I was a stranger and you welcomed me' (Matt. 25:33).

(b) A Theology of Brother- and Sisterhood and of Human Development

In an Africa in which development in general preoccupies us a great deal, the question of human development takes on a capital importance. We are more and more convinced that the Christian faith will be imperilled not by dogmatic belief but by failure to act as we need to act. The message of African theology is plain: *the service of developing the whole person is an integral part of the message of the Gospel.* For us proclaiming the Gospel involves promoting the development of human beings in all their dimensions as sons and daughters of God. It follows that the socio-political, economic and cultural dimensions of every human creature cannot be cut off from their religious dimension. This fits in with the best of African anthropology, that is to say, its sense of the unity between the 'profane world' and the 'sacred world', on the one hand, and, on the other, its sense of being human as a mystery of solidarity and communion. In saying this we do not mean to overlook the fact that this African vision of the world and of human beings is being severely shaken by the emergence of new problems, for example, industrialisation, urbanisation, demographic expansion, modern science and technology, not to mention secularisation and atheistic materialism. We believe, however, that this vision of the world is still a vital reality deep down in the hearts of most Africans, the peasants and workers of Africa.

Today more than ever the *Church in Africa must become the voice of those without a voice* and take up the defence of these elements in being human that constitute the basis and ground of human life. The Church must pit itself with all its strength against everything that diminishes the human person, foments injustice, violence, oppression, the exaltation of blood and race, war and all that it brings about.[10]

It is important to note that the attention given to the theme of liberation in Africa is not restricted to political, economic and social conditions alone. African theologians are talking more and more about *anthropological poverty*. They have in mind a radical poverty, much graver than simply material poverty—the poverty that consists in stripping a human being not only of what s/he has but of everything that goes to make up her or his very being and dignity: his or her identity, history, being rooted in a particular ethnic group, her or his language, culture, faith, creativity, ambitions, right of speech ...

It is in this light that we have to see the explanation of the profound sympathy that African thinkers have for the theologies of liberation. We are against every sort of oppression because the Gospel of Jesus Christ require us to take part in the struggle to free people from every form of dehumanisation. This is why African theology seeks to put into practice the solidarity of Africans with Black Americans, Asiatics, Latin Americans, as well as all those who are fighting for a full human existence.

We can see what is at stake. The masses of Africa today are very sensitive to the values of justice, peace and solidarity. Without action in this direction evangelisation will lose a great deal of its credibility. But this is not all, and it is not going far enough. Working for justice and transforming the world are part and parcel of proclaiming the Gospel. This is where Christians and non-Christians can meet, this is a privileged place of dialogue and solidarity, a sign of the authentic love that is at the heart of the message of the Gospel.

Such is the task of the Church in Africa today. It amounts to *nothing less than changing the world*, giving meaning and value to the fight for justice by tying it to the whole revelation of the design of God in Jesus Christ, by bringing to it a certainty based on faith in the salvation accomplished by the Passion and Resurrection of Jesus Christ. As J. M. Ela writes, the Church in Africa 'is confronted with a duty to be vigilant, it is invited to have courage ... It must leave the well trodden paths of a behaviour that makes it remain a sort of dogmatic somnambulist among the violations of human beings, blind outrages, mutilations, structures of inequality and domination holding peoples in the grip of the tentacles of the neo-colonial system, perpetrated with the complicity of bureaucracies of power, while the insolent and scandalous affluence of a tiny group of privileged people induces the beggary of the vast majority of young and adult people'. And he goes on to add: 'If it wants to be part of the present history of Africa, the Church must understand that its identity is at stake at all levels of African society, where thousands of young Africans cannot turn their backs on the masses of the peasants and workers from whom they stem in order to join the club of the haves who live from the exploitation of the disinherited. It is with people thwarted of their rights, reduced to silence by State terrorism, threats and intimidation that the Church must become one flesh if it is truly the body of the Crucified one of Golgotha; it has to go back to where people really are but, once there, do everything it can to demonstrate its refusal to perpetuate the misery of our people. This is what the salvation of Jesus Christ means today, salvation through the only one who counts for us, submerged as we are in the sub-human conditions that many convergent factors impose on Africa.'[11]

(c) An Ecumenical Theology

African theology, we see, is *fundamentally ecumenical*. In Africa we are very conscious of the problem of the unity of Christians. The unity of Africa, like that of the world, is in some sort tied to the visible unity of Christians in one faith. This unique faith is our response to the unique Word of God proclaimed in the unique Jesus Christ. And it is terrible to think that Black Africa has been condemned by history to know only the divided Christ.[12]

For us ecumenism is not a diplomatic process for attaining good relations between Christian confessions. It is an *inner requirement of our faith*. There is not nor can there be Christian fidelity where people do not suffer from these divisions, due as they are for the most part to cultural failures to understand and forms of imperialism. The churches of Africa must do everything to avoid the resentment and rancour from which the churches that founded and evangelised them suffered and still do suffer. Thank God, the differences between Christian denominations among us have not attained the proportions they have in Europe. Africans have simply embraced the form of Christianity they were offered (Catholic, Anglican or Protestant) without always being aware of the origin of the division within the Church. This is why different Christian denominations among us experience less difficulty in collaborating. Our ecumenism refuses to engage in controversies, out of a desire to conduct a serene and humble search into the meaning of the Gospel message for our peoples. All of us, Catholic and Protestant, are invited to ask ourselves about what we have discovered and understood in regard to Christ and his message. We have to work together to see how we can proclaim Jesus Christ effectively to Africa today and tomorrow. Collaboration already exists in several fields: social progress, religious education, the translation of the Bible and theological research.

The Church's dialogue in Africa is about non-Christians, in particular about adherents of *traditional African religions and Islam*. In spite of the colonial experience and its system of depersonalisation, the religions of Africa retain a great deal of their vitality. They are the channels of great religious riches: a spiritual vision of life, a profound sense of God, of the family, of life after death, etc.[13]

Similarly in regard to Islam what needs to be emphasised is the number of elements common to Christianity and Islam, particularly belief in a single God and the sense of fraternity.[14]

Seen and analysed in this way, theology is completely of a piece with the 'post-missionary' Church in Africa. A church under tutelage but striving to be autonomous. In sum, African theology is a continual reflection on the mystery of the Church and on the world as these two are grasped in their existential and historical unity, an organic symbiosis between Christian tradition and contemporary reflection on what is at issue in the historical situation in which we find ourselves. This has direct consequences on theological language.

3. THE TRUE QUESTION: ASSUMING THE DIVERSITY OF CULTURES AND CIVILISATIONS

I regret not being able to develop these observations further, but they do add up to a radical question about the *true universality of the Church of Jesus Christ*. It is a serious question. At the same time, it is not an entirely new one. From its very beginnings Christianity experienced the test and the tension of unity and diversity. It expressed itself first in Aramaic, then in Greek, the genius of which is profoundly different from that of Aramaic. But what, in certain respects, seems new is the possibility of acknowledging and validating this diversity on a far greater scale, of envisaging a pluralism as wide as the world itself.[15]

The reservations about such a pluralism and the objections to it seem to stem, in large measure at any rate, from *too sharp an opposition between unity and pluralism*. Now to us this opposition seems to be at the very least superficial, and certainly accidental. It derives no doubt from the fact that the relationship between these two concepts has not been sufficiently clarified or well enough defined. Do we need to be more precise?

Theology is a reflection on the content of faith. We have already observed in passing that theological understanding is very complex in character. It presupposes, on the one hand, the divine testimony of revelation and, on the other, the use of the rational functions. This shows straight away that faith as much as reason directs theological reflection towards an objective synthesis that is universal in character. Grounding itself, on the one hand, on the identity of the revelation totally given in the person of Jesus Christ and, on the other, on the universality of the principles of the human spirit, theology faces the task of penetrating the divine mystery in such a way as to seize its deepest significance, as St Paul says: 'May the Father, according to the riches of his glory, grant you to be strengthened with might through his Spirit in the inner man, and that Christ may dwell in your hearts through faith; that you, being rooted and grounded in love, may have power to comprehend with all the saints what is the breadth and length and height and depth, and to know the love of Christ which surpasses knowledge, that you may be filled with all the fullness of God' (Eph. 3:16–19).

Far from opposing each other, unity and plurality call for and complete each other by way of a sort of intimate and reciprocal causality. A community of faith, a diversity of teaching. People too often have an inexact and incomplete idea of things when they think of this diversity as if it always possessed the same intensity and rigorous exclusiveness. It is nothing of the sort, even though one does have to admit, unhappily, that characteristics originally found to be original do degenerate into theological oppositions and even into schism.

What is in question is variations of emphasis which are not important enough to put our community of faith in question on such or such a question but which express themselves, at the level of thought as well as at that of the external manifestations of the Christian life (worship, ethical behaviour, institutions ...), in terms of notable differences that give each particular church a markedly distinctive configuration. At the same time we cannot hide the difficulties raised by the integration of the Gospel with cultures other than the Western one. Pius XII's saying is still valid: the Gospel stands in the midst of *all* cultures like a cultivated stem among wild trees.

Having said this, we must nevertheless go on to assert more vehemently than ever that the divine message is addressed to the whole world. It can be *proclaimed and understood in any language whatever*, as it has been in Greek, Latin, French, German or Russian. Provided only that it safeguards the unity of faith (*fides quae creditur*), a theology that expresses itself in Arabic, Chinese or Bantu would be authentic theology. God no longer talks and deals with a chosen race or people but with the entire human race.[16] This dialogue centred on Christ the redeemer can continue only if Christianity presses all cultures of the world into service. The Church is Catholic not only because it brings truth to all peoples, at all times, but also because it requires the support of all civilisations, the contribution of all human beings if it is to bring to light all the riches that have been deposited with her and to build the eternal city of God. This is in accordance with the explicit teaching of Vatican II; this calls for theological reflection to be undertaken and encouraged in every socio-cultural region in such a way as to take into account the philosophies and wisdom of the peoples of the world.[17]

One last remark by way of conclusion. The time of self-contained civilisations cultivated as in a conservatory is past. Humanity is moving more and more towards a cosmic civilisation, built by human beings as a whole on the basis of fundamental common values. But *this universalisation is not uniformisation*. There will always be room, within this process of cultural unification, for a certain diversity. The universal civilisation will not rise on the graveyard of particular civilisations.

The bishops of Africa attach a great deal of importance to this principle, as they declared in 1974: 'In the spirit of that ecclesial communion to which Vatican II invited us, the bishops of Africa and Madagascar draw attention to the essential and fundamental role played by living Christian communities:

priests, religious and layfolk, united in thought and deed with their bishop. It is to such communities, incarnated and rooted in the life of their peoples that it falls in the first place to deepen the Gospel, to determine which pastoral objectives have priority, to take what initiatives mission calls for, and to discern, in faith, what elements of tradition can be preserved and what breaks have to be made in order to permit of a true penetration of all sectors of life by the Gospel.' And then went on to insist: 'Every action undertaken to construct our churches must be undertaken by constant reference to the life of our communities. It is from within these communities that we shall bring to the meeting place of catholicity not only our specific cultural and artistic experiences ... but a distinctive style of theological thinking that tries to respond to the questions put to us by different historical contexts and by the present evolution of our societies—theological thinking that is simultaneously faithful to the authentic tradition of the Church, attentive to the life of our Christian communities and respectful of our own traditions, our own languages, that is to say, our own philosophies' (see *Ad Gentes* § 22; *Unitatis Redintegratio* §§ 14 & 17).[18]

Translated by John Maxwell

Notes

1. This is how Pope John XXIII addressed the bishops of Africa when he received them in audience during the Council.

2. Cardinal B. Gantin 'Théologie africaine et catholicité' *Bull. de Théologie Africaine* 8, n. 8 (1982) 187.

3. H. Maurier 'Théologie africaine francophone' *Spiritus* n. 88 (1982) 227. See also our own contribution 'La verità nella Theologia Africana' in *Problemi e prospettive di teologia dogmatica* ed. K. H. Neufeld (Brescia 1983) pp. 445–469.

4. Here are a few titles: M. P. Hegba *Emancipation d'Eglises sous tutelle. Essai sur l'ère post-missionaire* (Paris 1976); E. Fashole-Luke, R. Gray *et al. Christianity in Independent Africa* (London 1978); *Libération ou adaptation? La théologie africaine s'interroge* (Paris 1979). A. Nolan *Jesus before Christianity* (London 1978); B. Adoukonou *Jalons pour une théologie africaine. Essai d'une herméneutique chrétienne du vodum dahomeen* (2 vols.) (Namur-Paris 1980); T. Tshibangu *La Théologie comme science au XXe siècle* (Kinshasa 1980); J. M. Ela *Le Cri de l'homme africain. Questions aux chrétiens et aux Eglises d'Afrique* (Paris 1980); O. Bimweny Kweshi *Discours théologique négro-africain. Problème des fondements* (Paris 1981); F. Eboussi Boulaga *Christianisme sans fétiche. Révélation et domination* (Paris 1981); A. T. Sanon and R. Luneau *Enraciner l'Evangile. Initiations africaines et pédagogie de la foi* (Paris 1982); E. J. Penoukou *Eglises d'Afrique. Propositions pour l'avenir (Paris 1984)*; E. Mveng *L'Afrique dans l'Eglise. Paroles d'un croyant* (Paris 1986).

5. M. M. Veigh 'Africa: The Understanding of Religion in African Christian Theologies' *Concilium* 136 (1980) 57 at p. 60. And see also G. Thils *En dialogue avec l"Entretien sur la foi'* (Louvain-la-Neuve 1986).

6. Witness the *Bulletin de Théologie Africaine*, the official organ of the Association Oecumenique des Théologiens Africains (AOTA). Since 1979 the review has appeared twice a year.

7. See the work of F. Eboussi Boulaga cited in note 4, at pp. 155–156.

8. *Combats pour un christianisme africain. Mélanges en l'honneur du Prof. V. Mulago* ed. A. Ngindu Mushete (Kinshasa 1981) is still worth referring back to.

9. See the work by O. Bimwenyi Kweshi cited in note 4, at pp. 386–387.

10. See *L'Eglise et la promotion humaine en Afrique aujourd'hui*. Exhortation pastorale du Symposium des Conférences Episcopales d'Afrique et de Madagascar (Kinshasa 1985).

11. J. M. Ela 'De l'assistance à la liberation. Les tâches actuelles de l'Eglise en milieu africain' *Foi et Developpement* n. 83–84 (1981) 4–5.

12. On the ecumenical movement in Africa see E. J. Penoukou *Eglises d'Afrique* pp. 107–126.

13. For the continuing life and presence of African religions, see *inter alia Les Religions africaines comme source de valeurs de civilisation* Colloque de Cotonou (16–22 August 1972) (Paris 1972); *L'Afrique et ses formes de vie spirituelle*. 2e. colloque international du Centre d'Etudes des Religions Africaines (CERA) (Kinshasa 1983).

14. See the excellent work of J. Jomier *L'Islam aux multiples aspects* (Kinshasa 1982).

15. On this point see a stimulating work: *Théologie et choc des cultures*. Colloque de l'Institut Catholique de Paris ed. C. Geffré (Paris 1984).

16. See the collective work of the International Theological Commission 'L'Unite de la foi et le pluralisme théologique' in *La Doc. Cath*. 63 (1966) col. 1740.

17. See in particular the decree *Ad Gentes* § 22.

18. 'Promouvoir l'évangelisation dans la corresponsabilité. Declaration des evêques d'Afrique et de Madagascar présents à la 4e Assemblée du Synode des Evêques' (1974) in *La Doc. Cath*. 1664 (1974) col. 995.

Joseph Moingt

'Oportet et Haereses Esse'

PAUL'S WELL-KNOWN declaration 'Oportet et haereses esse' (1 Cor.
11:19) loses much of its original, enigmatic character in most modern readings
(for example in the French translation of the Jerusalem Bible, which runs: 'Il
faut bien qu'il y ait aussi des scissions parmi vous'. Or as James Moffatt
translates it: 'There must be parties among you (if geniune Christians are to be
recognised)'). For Paul wrote of 'heresies', not of 'parties' or 'divisions'. But
the Church Fathers found in the words that followed, 'so that those who are in
the right may be recognised' matter for soothing comments of a pastoral or
spiritual nature which enabled them to skirt the *mysterious necessity of a
perpetual resurgence of heresies in the Church*. In these days we are more on our
guard against totalitarian, uniformising talk, more anxious to make clear our
special viewpoints and differences; we might even be tempted to restore to the
Apostle's declaration its provocative force and use it as a justification of the
right to differ, to engage in verbal confrontation and constructive challenges,
which would give a new meaning to the word 'heresy', something akin to
'creative rupture', an expression coined by my friend Michel de Certeau which
is certain to gain wide currency. Changes in the meanings of words justify such
endeavours to introduce fresh readings. But before elaborating some new
interpretation we should do well to try to see whether Paul's plain intention to
forbid 'I praise you not': 'I condemn') what he calls *schismata* or *haereses* can
be turned, otherwise than by caprice, into an encouragement of 'divergence',
and whether history offers any basis for this endeavour.

1. THE TRIAL OF FAITH

The dissensions with which Paul reproached the Corinthians—*schismata*,

64

scissuras (v. 18)—signify *breaks in the fellowship of Christians*, not differences of faith. There is therefore no basis for the assertion of many exegetes that he has in mind a different kind of division when he adds: *dei gar kai haireseis einai—nam oportet et haereses esse* (*v. 19*). However, it must be conceded to those same interpreters that the phrase denotes a gradation (*kai—et*) which gives a stronger meaning to the second word, that of a real break or rent in Church unity. Paul finds that there are some disturbances in the Church, but that does not upset him, because he foresees that even more serious divisions will occur later on: 'there must *even* be rending and tearing off'. These disorders may originate in disagreements in the faith, and this might well be foreseen in a religious society. But there were then, as there always are, a great many other causes of division, for example those 'parties'—*schismata*—formed around different leaders of the community at Corinth (1 Cor. 1.10), to which Paul attaches an equal importance. The prominence he gives in this letter and in this context to the idea of 'the body of Christ' (1 Cor. 10:17; 11:29; 12:12) shows that he has mainly in mind, more than the causes of these disturbances, whatever they were, the result which would inevitably follow, if not at the time then later, namely the *'dismemberment' of the body of Christ which is his Church.*

What *time scale* has the Apostle in mind when he warns of such devastating events? Very probably he is thinking of *the coming of the last days*, which is the time horizon familiar to the New Testament writers. When Jesus spoke about this he used similar language: 'Scandals, stumbling blocks have to come' (Matt. 18:7); in the context of biblical language, he meant by that saying *trials of faith*, not errors concerning the 'mysteries' enunciated by dogma, but, more fundamentally (more seriously?) the test of that confidence in salvation which we owe to God and his Christ and of the discernment of the true God and true Christ, a trial capable of causing even the elect to stumble and drag down many another with themselves (Matt. 24:24). Among these 'signs' of the last days which will be stumbling blocks, Jesus pointed to people 'betraying one another and hating one another' (Matt. 24:10) even within the same family (Luke 12:52–3; Matt. 10:35). In Paul's text the eschatological perspective (often misunderstood) is made explicit by the reference to the 'trial' of faith (*dokimoi*, see v. 28), this being the immanent action of God's judgment, which the present dissensions are in danger of incurring (*krima*, vv. 29 and 34), and by the reference to the 'manifestation' (*phaneroi*) which will follow it. This too will be a work of God, when 'the Lord will reveal (*phanerosei*) life's inner aims and motives' (1 Cor. 4:5) 'for we all have (*dei*) to appear without disguise before the tribunal of Christ' (2 Cor. 5:10).

Both the necessity (*dei*) of which Paul speaks and that announced by Jesus in the Gospels (*dei*) of his passion and resurrection, are *eschatological in nature, the result of a divine purpose*, announced in veiled terms in the Scriptures; it refers directly to the trial and the manifestation of faith ('there must be ... if') and not to the 'divisions' (however understood) which are only the instruments of this testing; and the threat hanging over these troublemakers is not that of being arraigned before a 'human tribunal', but God's; for 'it is the Lord who cross-questions me on the matter ... He it is who will come to bring dark secrets to the light ...' (1 Cor. 4:3–5). Paul frequently (as here) urges the faithful to prepare themselves for this divine judgment by 'testing themselves', both individually and as a community (1 Cor. 11:28: *dokimazeto*). But he warns them against the temptation to usurp God's place by judging others: 'the hour of reckoning has still to come' (1 Cor. 4:5). The test of time is needed for the trial of faith, and this is to be done in a fraternal dialogue in which none is forbidden to have his say, everyone is assured of a respectful hearing, and all are called to a mutual 'discernment'. 'Never quench the fires of the spirit, never disdain prophetic revelations but test them all (*dokimazete*), retaining what is good' (1 Thess. 5:19–21). Hasty, partisan judgments, which give rise to divisions within a community, can be avoided only if all are 'united in a common temper and attitude' (1 Cor. 1:10).

This analysis *in no way devalues the exercise of teaching authority in the Church*. Paul, of all people, provides some telling examples of that vocation. It does not call for some 'right to be mistaken', or 'in schism', or 'heretical'. It does however highlight the obligation to allow one's faith to be tested, to allow time for this to happen, and space in which to exercise it; the obligation to engage in dialogue within the Church, to acknowledge the right of everyone to speak, to speak differently from others, and to allow the necessary time for the truth to be made manifest in a fraternal, prophetic critical dialogue ('discernment').

By the same token it warns those who have authority to speak against depriving others of that right, making the trial of faith *instead of* others, so monopolising a responsibility which is laid upon each person individually and upon all in common. It alerts them against the risk of themselves becoming instruments of division, by 'anticipating the time' of God's judgment (*pro kairou*) by untimely action, instead of waiting for the Lord's arrival (1 Cor. 4:5).

2. THE BIRTH OF AN ORTHODOXY

During the first period of the Christian era, roughly the first three centuries, Paul's advice, as we have interpreted it, was put into practice. Present-day historical exegesis enables us to see the great *diversity of doctrines and practices which coexisted in the apostolic communities without destroying communion in the faith.* This situation persists during the second century, when there lived side by side in a single church or province, without clear lines of demarcation and without anathematising one another, some more or less judaizing Christians, and 'Ebionites' who acknowledge hardly, if at all, the divine sonship of Jesus, Pauline Christians more or less 'antilegalist' and 'Marcionites' in the process of rejecting the Old Testament, believers trained by the old presbyters and 'gnostics' subject to a foreign religious rule, more or less rigorous practicants and sectarian 'Encratists', vaguely anarchist charismatics and 'Montanists' who were shortly to go over to schism. The doctrinal polemics which appear towards the middle of the second century indicate that a 'discernment' was taking place, in which a right of speech was being exercised, and their persistence until the beginning of the fourth century proves that faith was allowed sufficient time to test the truth and *to progress from confrontation to consensus.*

Irenaeus' habit, followed by the ancient 'heresiologists', of attaching suspect doctrines to pagan philosophies shows that the word 'heresy' long retained its classical, secular meaning of a philosophical school, religious sect or political party. Not until a consensus was formed within the Church did it acquire its *'canonical' connotation of a departure from the rule of faith.* The Councils held throughout the third century sketched out the main lines of this consensus around the preaching of bishops, the heritage of a tradition; but what Cyprian said shows that the churches were not yet ready to accept either a supra-episcopal authority, that of a majority at a Council or that of a see having the primacy, or to give up their local traditions and unify them under the auspices of a centralising administration. Until that time, *responsibility for 'discernment' of doctrines and practices was left to a dialogue of the faithful, theologians and bishops.* This dialogue often involved controversy and sometimes bitter confrontation, but in the end it did what was needed since Marcionism, Ebionism, Gnosis, Encratism and Montanism were on the way to extinction or peaceful rejection by the beginning of the fourth century, without any other kind of procedure.

It is clear that, after Nicaea, the *ecumenical councils changed the procedure* and introduced an idea of 'orthodoxy' that was *no longer consensual but authoritarian.* It was then that they began not only to denounce but also to suppress and root out 'heresy' with all the powers available to a hierarchical institution. On this subject we shall confine ourselves to some empirical observations which do not call for erudite discussion, without taking sides on a history which has attracted its full meed of scholarly comment.

In many instances, what was condemned as 'heresy' started out purely as a theological opinion, linked to a current of philosophical thought, and having little currency outside restricted intellectual circles (consider, for example, the beginnings of Arianism). Or else it began with some insufficiently elaborated conceptual terms which were misunderstood in differing cultural contexts (the *miephusis* is an example recognised today). In other cases it was the reaction against learned terms recently introduced or disseminated, which might be in conflict with local traditions (the famous 'new words' of Nicaea, the *theotokos*). In many cases, both camps were equally determined to maintain the received faith, and both had about an equal mixture of clarities and obscurities, of upright intentions and crooked concealed motives. Both also had many highly respected persons on their side, until one side won, perhaps owing to the play of ecclesiastical or political power. These few observations scarcely allow us to depict the struggles of orthodoxy against heresy as apocalyptic combats between good and evil, truth and the lie: let us leave them on the plane of historical contingency. Let us accept, on principle, that the condemnations pronounced were, in their context, justified. *But how effective were they?*

Seldom did they achieve the desired result, which was the rapid disappearance of the heresy in question. For example, survivals of Arianism or other christological heresies are found late in the Western Middle Ages in the guise of 'adoptionism' or 'opinions' taught in the universities: denouncing the error had not sufficed to enlighten the minds. Far more serious is the fact that by their canonical and political consequences, and their psychological and cultural effects, those condemnations *precipitated the creation of churches separated from catholicity, Nestorian or Monophysite*; later came the disastrous East–West schism, and later still the tragic division of Western Christianity. All these 'schisms' remain until this day, without the 'heresy' which was denounced having been extirpated. A heavy price has been paid for 'purifying' the faith, and in the end the *unity of the faith, remade with each condemnation, has become very ambiguous*, because the Catholic Church has suceeded in clothing itself in the mantle of infallibility from one Council to another only at the cost of severing from itself large portions of the people of God. The 'dismemberment' glimpsed and dreaded by Paul has not been avoided.

Was it avoidable? *Could the error have been 'denounced' without 'condemning' the persons*, without banishing entire provinces from the Church? Could the truth have been rediscovered peacefully (evangelically!) without loosing anathemas bringing in their train acts of sacrificial violence? Perhaps the times were not propitious. It must be remembered that the birth of a formal orthodoxy was contemporary with the birth of the Christian empire, which had the same need as the old pagan empire to reinforce its political unity with a religious bond, and as many reasons as the Church for imposing a universal discourse of communication by force. The unity of the faith and of the church was seldom the only thing at stake when heresies were condemned; it was not always either the main causative factor or the principal gain.

The political situation of the Church is quite different today. Is a different mode of fellowship and of serving the truth, other than militant orthodoxy, thinkable now?

3. FELLOWSHIP IN THE TRUTH

A different sense of the fellowship of believers in an identical Christian faith has already appeared. Ways of thinking have moved on, giving rise to new practices within the Church. Catholics, including pastors and theologians, are meeting with 'separated Christians' from the East or the West, without feeling that they are in contact with 'dangerous heretics' or rebel 'schismatics', as these terms were understood in past centuries. The sting has been drawn from the old rivalries. *Differences of belief and practice have been relativised.* We no longer live in religious societies, where the truth follows geographical boundary lines, and where the words and gestures of a group and the prescriptions of an authority were regarded as sacred precepts or prohibitions. Unanimity of doctrine and practice is no longer demanded even within the confines of a single church. On the contrary, all alike experience the same differences or disputes, the same uncertainties about fundamental tenets, the same failures in the Christian life, and similar disobedience towards the most official teachings. Can we profess ignorance, and say that heresy or schism is found only outside our own church? In such a situation, more meaning is attached to basic attitudes and commitment of life than to words and ceremonies, greater importance to the Gospel than to formulations almost unknown to the people, and we rejoice to feel ourselves in fellowship on the essentials of the faith.

Demarcation lines have shifted and become permeable. Has this effectively done away with the ancient situation of heresy of schism? Suspicion is still vigilant within the Catholic hierarchy, as doubtless also in other churches, but it is turned inwards as much as outwards. Ecumenism receives encouragement—accompanied by warnings about the dangers of 'doctrinal relativism' to which it might lead. A loss or lessening of the 'feeling for truth' is feared. Is such a fear justified? Yes, if it is thought that knowledge of the truth can be totally divorced from the contingencies of history, politics, culture and so on, and that if proclaimed by a competent religious authority truth is freed from those contingencies. But such an idea is no longer compatible with modern epistemologies. Must modern minds be blamed for being conditioned differently from those of past centuries? In truth, it is the claim to a universal, atemporal truth which nowadays merits the reproach of a lack of respect for truth, and religious authorities should take urgent note of this. On the other hand, there is no need to fear a loss of the feeling for truth if one has an eschatological vision of revealed truth, a humbler estimate of our ability to know truth in itself and a more critical historical sense, and if a confession of faith is not confused with the formulations in which it is expressed to meet the needs of a given society at a given epoch. Catholic definitions of the truth have always been defensive reactions of the body social against what is perceived as an attack. This polemical interrelation restricts the scope of these definitions, as proclaimed, whilst the movement of historical parameters enables the quarrels of the past to be appraised more calmly, and facilitates a fresh approach to the truth once contested.

Heresy has for long been defined, according to its supposed etymological derivation, as the 'choice' which accepts one point in the rule of faith and rejects another. Nowadays, however, we are more aware of the 'kernel of truth' contained in every heresy, and of the danger of losing that kernel by condemning the heresy. It is fact that, taken in the historical context in which it arises, 'heresy' is usually a response to an intention of faith and is meant to affirm that one doctrine forms part of the faith rather than to deny its opposite. *The contest between orthodoxy and heresy is a confrontation between two traditions*, one older or more widespread, the other more recent or having a more restricted orientation, and the one that becomes the champion of the truth is not always the one which was originally the older or the more widespread belief. Orthodoxy too is a 'choice', and all choices are impoverishing. Therefore although the 'ecumenism' of truth may carry a risk, it is first and foremost an opportunity of enrichment for churches previously opposed.

But it is not very satisfactory to be content with the idea of a truth of the faith which could be broken down into a number of parts, some common to all the churches whilst others are dispersed among them all, and might be combined with errors which run counter to the truths held by all. In heterodoxy and orthodoxy alike, the faith forms a system. *Every doctrinal and religious system is a coherent vision of the faith, but seen from a different, special point of view*, with varying degrees of openness or closedness.

Vatican II gave currency to the idea of *a hierarchy of articles of faith. This contains the germ of a new epistemology*, and it ought to be applied to every one of the articles, because the structure of the whole is reflected in the way the different propositions constituting one and the same dogma are articulated, and this too is hierarchical. If this were adopted, no longer would the camp of truth be set against the camp of error; no longer would the truths and errors assignable to each camp be totted up against one another. Instead the idea of 'differing truths', or rather of differing constellations of the one truth of the faith, would take over.

This new epistemology should alter the way in which the ecumenical dialogue is conducted. Instead of confronting one another across the fault lines produced by history, and vainly seeking to bridge them, a synchronous, organic understanding of the different constellations of faith would reveal the communion which exists at the summit of the structures and would enable it to be extended downwards, down to the lower levels where the truth is fractured. For it would no longer be a case of each one being satisfied with his own truth and respecting the other's truth so long as he did not have to share it. Truth would be no less at stake than in the battles of the past, but it would be more authentic. The truth of the faith is actuated by *charity* and not by the desire to be proved right at somebody else's expense. Charity means sharing the truth with others, so that the unity of the faith may be built up. But the unity created by charity is not the uniformity of a social, political or religious order. *It rejoices in the diversity which each loves to discover in the other* when s/he recognises, full of promise and demand, the same truth that is in him or her.

4. THE SERVICE OF THE FAITH

But the problem of relationships between an orthodoxy and a heterodoxy is no longer posed only in terms of relationships between one confession and another, for henceforth *it will be found within each one*, as we have already mentioned, no longer in the guise of a declared, duly documented conflict between two denominations, but of a war of movement between a body of official doctrine and a divided, diversified public opinion. These two problems can no longer be resolved separately; they call for understanding and a sympathetic attitude from those in authority.

During the last few decades a new and geographically widespread phenomenon has appeared in the Catholic Church (and other churches): many of the faithful, whilst breaking free from the traditions and rules of religious practice, *have given up the habit of submission towards the teaching authority and received doctrines*; other laymen, in increasing numbers, felt they had become 'enlightened', 'grown up' believers and wished to behave as being responsible for their own understanding of the faith and of church affairs, learning theology, making their voices heard, and not afraid to come out publicly against authoritative pronouncements. Many theologians have left the well worn paths of institutional teaching. They have been rethinking old problems and posing new ones, distancing themselves from the instructions of the hierarchy, listening to and serving the currents of opinion in the Church. Then again the media take up these questionings and independent views, and this has strengthened and amplified the new phenomenon of a theology in the making, in the open air, in many places where responsible answers to current problems are being thrashed out under the gaze of the public at large.

Authority tends to react to this new phenomenon along the lines of the ancient heresiologies; the origins of these currents of thought are sought in the human sciences, as formerly in the philosophical schools. It is shown that they have already been condemned with modernism, as once previous Councils of the Church were cited for authority. Priests guilty of leading the people astray were denounced, as were once the doctors who misled 'simple folk'. The hierarchy would rather close its eyes to the new things that are happening, so as not to have to change the old attitudes of the teaching authority. But 'choosing' the old in preference to the new involves a serious risk of enlarging and multiplying the 'schisms' it is hoped to heal. *The time seems ripe for a return to 'testing' and 'discerning' the faith.* What is being questioned is neither the existence of an authoritative word nor its legitimacy, but its *mode of operation*. For long its function has been to compensate for the inability of those who were variously called 'simple', 'unlettered' or 'ignorant' to speak. For long its use has been to prevent unorthodox doctrines from sowing discord.

But in these days, to clamp down on dissentient expression would be to silence all speech, and that would end not in reestablishing harmony but in frustrating the best intentions and, at the very least, creating silent dissent within the Church. In the present situation, characterised both by democratic freedoms and widespread unbelief, it is vitally necessary for Christians to think through their own beliefs, to speak to one another about them, to seek new ways of expressing them and to engage in free, public discussion of them. The vitality of the faith depends upon the 'trial' of communication and scrutiny.

This being the case, the *teaching authority is called to find a different way of operating in the service of the faith*, to guide research, to illuminate 'discernment', consciously to listen to 'what the Spirit is saying to the churches', to enter into dialogue, to welcome discussion, to encourage prophetic speech, to promote fellowship without blurring differences.

In an age when authoritative pronouncements no longer have the power to create unity, the message of the Apostle comes across with fresh relevance: Differences must be allowed to surface in order that, by the test of time and the word, by consultation and comparison, the truth of the faith may become manifest in the light of charity.

Translated by Alan Braley

Tiemo Rainer Peters

Orthodoxy in the Dialectic of Theory and Practice

CONSIDERED TRADITIONALLY, orthodoxy arises where the faith is proclaimed by the infallible teaching authority, is transmitted by the right kind of theology and preaching, and is accepted obediently by the faithful. This presupposes what is to be the main theme of what follows: the idea that *history and historical practice are constitutive for the category of Christian* doxa *or opinion.* In particular the teaching primacy, if it does not want to land itself in complete contradiction to Vatican I's criticism of traditionalism, is indeed not just an instrument for establishing what the truth is but also one for its continued creative formation. The most recent council made this connection clear when it emphasised the teaching infallibility that belongs to the Church as a whole before dealing with the plenary power and infallibility enjoyed by the hierarchy. Together with the Church's teaching office the 'people of God' possess a *sensus fidei* which cannot err (*Lumen gentium* § 12):[1] a historical, creative foundation upon which faith and life, theory and practice seek and articulate their unity.

The council was quite obviously concerned with biblical foundations and with making itself understandable to a modern age which in the wake of the Enlightenment associated 'tradition' and 'authority' with the epithet 'feudal' and rejected them on that account. The following contribution to fundamental theology is also concerned with *both fidelity to the biblical witness and coming to an understanding with the modern age.* The semantically enigmatic Greek concept *doxa,* nowhere firmly established in the New Testament and meaning 'opinion' or 'teaching' in the changing succession of time, hides a plethora of theological meanings: gnosis, kerygma, dogma, *veritas catholica*, etc. The dialectical relationship of these to practice, and more precisely their discussion in connection with the specifically modern dialectic of theory and practice, is the subject which, as will be shown, has a background which is very much rooted both in contemporary history and in contemporary life.

1. THE JEWISH INHERITANCE

In Judaism the continuity of the faith was represented as a very *this-worldly relationship of life and loyalty*. What is later to be meant by orthodoxy has its roots here, even if the concept (and not just the concept) has a Greek definition. Christian orthodoxy can only be understood along with that great historical movement yearning for salvation and liberation. Yahweh is its protagonist and guarantor; the covenant its milieu; living according to the law its content.

This needs underlining because everything else follows from it. The Judaeo-Christian idea of God cannot be considered, thought of or understood *in isolation from action*. It is practical in itself and is beyond the reach of objectification. What is involved is a God 'who is not God if you comprehend him' (Przywara).

Almost precisely the opposite applied in the Greek Enlightenment. 'God' is in itself a theoretical idea, the goal of a cosmos that discloses itself in the transcendental act of speculation. This state of astonished contemplation of the divine is termed immortal by Aristotle, whereas the mortal realm of the social, historical and political is delivered over to the most variegated polytheism. Independently of theoretical monotheism it was this latter that determined practical behaviour and immediate interests.[2] This was a consequence of a Platonism and idealism following which the people were not really to be taken seriously in theological matters, nor were their idols to be taken seriously theologically.

In contrast to this the Judaeo-Christian God is 'known' or recognised less by a process of theoretical assurance than by means of *historical experience and dialogue*—and then not as a hovering cosmic indifference to the gods of power as it is exercised and of everyday interests but as the personification of involvement, as the liberator from idols and the anti-idol. 'Hear, o Israel!' Heterodoxy, therefore, as far as its fundamental structure is concerned is leaving the messianic history of salvation, the demand for signs rather than being prepared for exodus, the hankering after strange gods.

2. WITNESSING TO CHRIST

Despite all one's reservations about making such an approximation too soon, it can be said that in primitive Christianity orthodoxy, which arises not at the periphery but at the centre of the truth of faith, where it is a question of the meaningfulness of salvation,[3] is nothing other than *witnessing to Christ*, which means imitating and following him in discipleship. And this points to a dialectic which Dietrich Bonhoeffer summed up by saying: 'Only the believer is obedient and only the person who is obedient believes.'[4]

In the Gospel—which itself can only be properly heard and read to the extent that it is followed—it is quite clear that one's first steps towards imitating and following Christ are at the same time one's first steps towards faith. There is no kind of delay that is not at the same time a keeping away from faith (Matt. 8:18–22) and no faith that does not at once lead to following Jesus (Matt. 19:16–22). The Easter faith already possesses a similar structure: nothing to indicate that the disciples were merely the passive recipients of information from outside. Nevertheless it should be emphasised that the resurrection was not generated by faith but instead generated faith. But this 'causality' took place completely beyond the temporal (earlier and later) or hierarchical (above and below) patterns of Greek philosophy or its pattern of theory and practice. It was rather of a dialectical nature and established a *logos* that can only be grasped or comprehended practically, in the *process of change or metanoia*;[5] that of the suffering, powerless Messiah who is yet present beyond and despite his death and calling people to discipleship.

The *community of Corinth*, rather far removed from such apocalyptic experiences and expectations, followed a different resurrection faith: one that was 'purer' and took on a Hellenistic tinge, that managed without recalling the powerless man who was crucified and that identified the happenings of Easter with Christ's entry into his dominion at the end of time. Time and history were now virtually obliterated and the practical demands of discipleship were side-stepped in gnostic fashion. One could stand the language of the later prologue of St John's gospel on its head and say: 'The flesh became word.'

What seemed like a radicalised orthodoxy was for Paul nothing other than 'the worship of idols' (1 Cor. 10:14) and the misrepresentation of God (1 Cor. 15:15). Faith in the resurrection is only really orthodox when it is lived as introducing one into the broken 'impure' relationships of suffering and death that are in need of redemption (1 Cor. 15:58). Without this practice *doxa* would merely be an indication of false faith and the most edifying celebrations of the Eucharist nothing but a meal at 'the table of demons' (1 Cor. 10:21). But in order to be able to put this view forward Paul has to formulate the correct *gnosis*: the awkward, 'foolish' and profoundly apocalyptic message of the crucified one who has been raised up (1 Cor. 15).

3. THE JOHANNINE IMPULSE

In the third Christian generation the *embellishments of recollection and eschatological hope began to suppress apocalyptic yearning.* The faith was handed on in a more official, more liturgical, more churchy form.[6] Doctrine now became the container of truth after its original bearers, the community of *Marána tha*, 'Our Lord, come' (1 Cor. 16:22), had begun to lose certainty and stability. The real age of orthodoxy had started.

However necessary it was for Christianity, at least in its struggle against gnosticism, to express itself as a Church and to establish its teaching, equally important precisely at this time remained the *prophetic protest of Johannine theology*. The fact that John too is concerned about orthodoxy is shown by the programmatic way in which the fourth gospel argues against the docetic gnosis and thus anticipates every theology of God's self-communication: 'The word became flesh' (John 1:14). Under this theological motto the historical presence of the revelation in Jesus is defended (John 14:6). This is done in such a way that at the same time the view is criticised that a presence of salvation exists only at the margins of the guaranteed knowledge of revelation, of the official doctrinal formula or of the authorised form of Church order. The history of the faith and of the 'witnesses' is itself a much clearer presence.[7]

The formula which John uses to present orthodoxy as practice as a corrective to orthodoxy as mere fidelity to official doctrine is: 'Abide in my love' (John 15:9). *Correct faith is this abiding.* Truth itself is born here if it is concerned to be alive, which means true in the Johannine sense of the word. Truth as unity and unity as love, not as organisational pressure, is then the summing up of what can and should be expressed as orthodoxy within the Johannine tradition.[8]

The *dangers of a free development* of this Johannine approach are obvious: the loss of the apocalyptic sense of time and justice; abandoning the historical Jesus and the Pauline idea of the crucified one who has been raised up; individualism, sectarian piety, gnosis. Every position in which practice is linked monistically with the claim to orthodoxy is bound sooner or later to run into these and similar dangers. The gospel according to St John itself stands, however, as a canonised corrective, against the opposite danger which in the course of Church history has certainly given rise to no less mischief: that of an indoctrinated Christianity and its 'pure doctrine' which is often as un-understood as it is not taken to heart and which appears with the claim to produce orthodoxy virtually automatically in the act of its obedient acceptance. This has become intolerable particularly for the modern mind. In this way the Johannine impulse, as the antithesis, is an aspect of that dialectic of theory and practice that is of fundamental importance precisely for an understanding of orthodoxy adequate for our age.

4. A 'TESTAMENT' FOR THE ENLIGHTENMENT

The problem of Johannine theology was that *faith must still be able to reach Jesus himself* even though, after Easter and in view of waning expectation of an imminent end of the world, it remains dependent on official transmission through the Church. Lessing was a heartfelt sharer of this view but could no longer see any way of establishing it. How could 'accidental truths of history' be turned into 'the proof of necessary truths of reason'?[9] By authoritarian and dogmatic imposition? Unthinkable for the Enlightenment. The Pauline idea of the crucified one who has been raised up—that 'demonstration of the Spirit and power' which could still be upheld against the gnostics of Corinth with the claim to orthodoxy (1 Cor. 2:4)—now has 'neither spirit nor power any longer' but has 'shrunk to human testimonies of spirit and power'. Jesus's resurrection has become completely unacceptable and has been exposed as 'a trick of the disciples' (Reimarus) or as a myth.

Thus opened up that 'horrible yawning gap' which has become well enough known from Lessing's defence of the writings of Reimarus and which seemed to make impossible any living link with tradition, with history, with biblical religion. The process began that we were to see as one of bourgeois rationality. Lessing himself concludes our text with a thoroughly pious wish, that 'everything that is divided by the gospel of John may be reunited again by the testament of John', adding: 'It is admittedly apocryphal, this testament, but none the less divine for that reason.'

Here, as a later dialogue explains,[10] the interest of the Enlightenment is linked with that presbyter of Ephesus who at the end could only talk of love. Our question is whether, in its struggle with authoritarianism and dogmatism, faith must necessarily do without all explicit *doxa*. That might have done in the community of Christians living in imminent expectation of the end. But in the wake of the assimilation of John by bourgeois society it was easy, as is shown by the legacies of theology up to our own day, for what for Paul was the foundation of any and every orthodoxy, the kerygma of the crucified one who has been raised up, to be demythologised and interpreted away as needed. *Faith became liberal, a matter of free choice*, in other words in the strict sense of the term *heretical*.[11]

5. THE DIALECTIC OF THEORY AND PRACTICE

While the thought of the modern age was making sure of its own requirements, a dialectic became visible that, not accidentally, showed itself to be supremely relevant and fruitful theologically.

Critical thought, with increasing radicalism from Kant via Hegel to Marx, saw the *essence of reason in freedom and liberation*. This happened with closer contact with both the biblical and the Greek tradition. Kant made it clear to the (theoretical) reason that it had to renounce the entire wealth of Greek theory (in the sense of pre-critical ontology) if it wished to be theory in the enlightened style of experience. *Reason itself*, once it liberated itself from ontological dogmatism, *became practical*, which for Kant meant as much as mature. It no longer discovered freedom as an idea under whose guidance it had to become practical but realised itself as freedom and in this hit on its own practical basic structure: the dialectic of theory and practice in its original form.[12] This 'Copernican turning point' (Kant) of modern thought had the consequence that practice no longer stood under the remote control and surveillance of theory. It became clear that theory first became plausible when seen from the point of view of practice, that it was only when viewed from this angle that thought became recognisable in its individuality as cognitive practice.

The practical observer no longer came from outside as theory had done in the past, with the result that the priorities had changed in the relationship between theory and practice. It was a matter of dialectic. Marx had recognised (and thereby provided a logical continuation of Kant's *Critique of Pure Reason*) that all knowledge and insight, even the purest and most enlightened, was swayed by other interests and thus had a practical orientation. Reason only became really free and rational when it recognised itself in its interests and could justify itself, when it reached the practical foundation of its discourse.

Johann Baptist Metz has shown how, standing under the primacy of the practical, modern thought has developed in the direction of post-idealistic concepts and has provided a foundation for theological reason.[13] With regard to truth its aims and objects are now finally of importance. The dialectic of theory and practice can be seen as an ethical and social one, as a movement (or history) directed at the subject and his or her interests, not only private but also public, not only spiritual but also material, not only immediate but also future, and always in the sense of his or her salvation, indeed redemption.

6. PRACTICAL ORTHODOXY

Most recently, at the point where modern and particularly Marxist dialectic shows its affinity for theology, theology has pointed out 'that the utopia of the liberation of everyone to become free agents in a manner worthy of human beings' would remain a mere projection 'if there were only utopia and no God' (Metz). It is, after all, no concession to Marx that faith has a practical orientation, has social obligations, is concerned with solidarity and can only be grasped in its truth on this basis. This follows from a Judaeo-Christian tradition from which the modern age, to the extent that it developed dialectic, has drawn its dynamism. But once allowed into theology and the Church the *thought of the modern age has once more brought the practical constitution of Christian discourse to the foreground*—at last.

God the liberator now emerges from the abstract ciphers encoded in the theory of grace. Dogmatics can be understood as the encoded history of a salvation: it demands a practical interpretation. The historical and social element of the gospels becomes clearly indispensable after it had seemed to have become almost lost (the quest for the historical Jesus). More important, it is attainable. We can become contemporaries of the historical Jesus. Following and imitating Christ, becoming his disciples, means this contemporaneity. It is the only suitable way of reading the Bible, what Clodovis Boff has called a practical reading, Benjamin a living exchange of experiences, Metz a central item of Christo-logy, Bonhoeffer participation in Jesus's being: in brief, *a practical orthodoxy*. The historical and technical reason, on the other hand, which destroys this kind of contemporaneity and has opened up the gulfs Lessing drew attention to, can be seen to be motivated by particular interests and emerges as the principle of bourgeois self-assertion and the erosion of solidarity.[14] Its truth is fundamentally identical with what pays.

The attempt to talk of orthodoxy under the modern age's primacy of practice can be made more precise by delving into *epistemology*. If within the dialectic of theory and practice truth makes itself known as conditioned by various interests, the question of truth must be given a new formulation that includes its political, social and material implications. It becomes: 'Are there interests that are capable of truth?'[15] Such interests exist when, and because truth is by definition universal only when, they are shown to be capable of being universal. The unconditional solidarity that is demanded in the Judaeo-Christian tradition corresponds to this kind of universality. Its goal is something which was called 'unity as love' in Johannine theology and was already in this context thought of as truth (John 3:21, 8:32) but which, because of the loss of the apocalyptic dimension in its radical universality that embraces love and justice, was no longer understood. But, seen in an apocalyptic perspective that covers the living and the dead, love possesses a totality that is of complete this-wordliness and complete transcendence and that makes it capable of truth in the sense of the dialectic of theory and practice.

This universality, which today is the subject of theological reflection under the label of 'anamnetic solidarity' or 'remembrance solidarity',[16] at the same time does away with dialectic in its material limitations (Lenin). The reason is that, as W. Benjamin has put it, the Christian understanding of truth refuses to regard 'history as fundamentally non-theological' and the past as locked away.[17] What becomes comprehensible is the extent to which that original apocalyptic proclamation of the resurrection of the crucified one and of the dead in general according to 1 Cor. 15 is the basis of any and every orthodoxy, and indeed why it is that practice, when understood in its radical sense, finds here its real foundation, one that can still only be expressed theologically. But this foundation or reason cannot be attained without practice: it does not exist without it, and without it it would be myth. This is one thing theology has been able to learn from the dilemmas of the Enlightenment.

What is involved is a *dialectic and not an identity of theory and practice*. However important the Johannine idea of unity and immediacy may be as a corrective, it must not be allowed to become the formal principle of orthodoxy. To make the identity of theory and practice one's starting point, for example by evoking the magic formula of orthopraxy, means ultimately suppressing the awkward otherness of suffering and death in a gnostic or monistic way, an otherness which is a constant irritant and stimulus to every Christian mode of action and which precisely but only in this way gives it its genuine intelligibility. Orthopraxy merely reproduces the blindness and rigidity of an orthodoxy that has no regard for practice. No practice can therefore realise what without practice would remain totally unreal and unthinkable: God's tension-filled and always open history of salvation in his dealings with men and women, something which is only recollected in a rough and ready way in Christian *doxa*. What exists as a pledge of any and every orthodoxy is valid practical ways of entering into this history. As always they are things like conversion, metanoia, discipleship, seeking first the kingdom of God (Matt. 6:33).

7. THE ORTHODOXY THAT IS DEMANDED

The question of the practical constitution of orthodoxy may be illuminated by the Enlightenment and by the modern age's dialectic of theory and practice, but it is only against the background of contemporary history that it becomes plausible and urgent.

(a) When *Dietrich Bonhoeffer* formulated his definition of discipleship in 1937 ('Only the believer is obedient and only the obedient person believes') this was also a slogan in the theological battle: against 'cheap grace', against orthodoxy as remaindered goods. In this way it was able to deal with a development that was particularly apparent in German fascism and that can still be encountered today: the idea that Christian doctrine should be kept 'pure' without the resulting orthodoxy leading to immediate mass protest on a Church-wide scale against barbaric rulers.

For Bonhoeffer it was clear that *orthodoxy represented a context of action and solidarity*—because 'God no longer wants to let himself be separated from his brother'.[18] Orthodoxy is 'expensive' if it wants to remain orthodox: it exists only on the side of those who suffer, in the living out of solidarity—to the point of martyrdom. The findings are rather unsettling: as far as Bonhoeffer was concerned indifference towards the victims of Nazism (particularly the Jews) meant not only that a shadow fell on the Christian churches (pleasanter times would return) but the entire structure of faith, the co-ordinates of orthodoxy, had become confused and muddled up. History and practice, the milieu and foundation of orthodoxy, could also become its grave. Hence Bonhoeffer demanded something that remains more than ever of the moment: 'All thinking, speaking and organisation in the affairs of Christianity must be reborn' from the 'prayer and action of the just among men and women'.[19]

(b) *Karl Rahner* has drawn attention to the existence of something like 'cryptogamous' heresy in the Church.[20] It does not take the form of explicit statements but corresponds to basic attitudes, interests and preferences which, however, if they were worked out according to their own logic, would be shown to be objectively heterodox. What is characteristic of this *structural heresy*, as it may also be termed, is that it surrounds itself, as it were, with orthodoxy, whether this out of traditional docility to the Church, a lack of civil courage in matters of religion and the Church, a lack of ability to adapt and assimilate the faith in terms of one's own life, indifference, or (a possibility Rahner does not mention) the calculation that religion can be useful and helps to establish the elements one approves of in structural heresy. If one understands Christian truth in its dialectical relationship to the practice of justice and love, the covert heresy envisaged by Rahner can be identified more precisely. It is to be found in the system of a structural injustice and apathy that completely determines, right down to the instinctive level (Marcuse), people's thinking, feeling and believing, particularly in wealthy industrialised societies. Without being recognised, alien gods intrude: not just orthodoxy but Judaeo-Christian monotheism is in danger.

This kind of distortion is prevented by genuine orthodoxy, which is not some half-heartedly supported alienating edifice but itself the support and indeed something like the dwelling-place of faith. This orthodoxy is not something one possesses but something one lives in, not in a purely spiritual or principled manner, nor in rigorous fidelity to principles and rules, but radically (Metz).

(c) The *Church of Medellín and Puebla* has strengthened the conciliar tendency towards the *teaching authority of the faithful* and has verified it in practice. Basic communities were discerned as places of theological production, the reading of the Bible by the humble was recognised as a source of knowledge of the faith, the poor were seen as 'evangelizatory potential' (Gutiérrez). Direct connections became possible. 'Faith and politics ask each other questions' (Clodovis Boff). Orthodoxy arises along the way of this questioning[21] and in this way shows itself to be no longer purely a problem of ideas but a problem of living. But what a way that is and what a life.

In this mutual questioning of faith and politics and in that living sharing of experience that takes place between the poor, the biblical narrators and the tradition of the faith, suffering above all else obtains a language. It is that which was first spelled out by the apocalyptic writers and which has unmistakably impressed itself on the Christian memory in Jesus's cry on the cross.

Orthodoxy then means first of all and primarily following the trace of this messianic revolt and longing. No dialectic reservation can relativise this kind of imminent expectation, and no one may divorce it from politics—even if it has been shown that even the fullest solidarity in practice is not immediately identical with the *veritas catholica* which points beyond the state of liberation that may have been reached at any one time to the entire history between death and resurrection. But for this reason no longer to take the earth and suffering seriously was something that already amounted to heresy in the case of the gnostics of Corinth, and how much more for many a 'Christian' cynic of today. 'Is Christ divided?' (1 Cor. 1:13).

Orthodoxy is indivisible. If it is not to turn out to be 'cheap' and structurally heretical it must hear the biblical demand for inclusive truth, a truth that embraces justice and love, and needs to ensure that it listens—universally. Orthodoxy is this obedience before it is anything else. And before any new name can be bestowed there is, for the source of any and every orthodoxy, already the old name full of promise, the people of God, or as the Council also put it the 'messianic people' (*Lumen gentium* § 9).

Translated by Robert Nowell

Notes

1. W. Beinert 'Bedeutung und Begründung des Glaubenssinnes (Sensus fidei) als eines dogmatischen Erkenntnisktriteriums' in *Catholica* 25 (1971) 293.

2. W. Pannenberg 'Die Aufnahme des philosophischen Gottesbegriffs als dogmatisches Problem der frühchristlichen Theologie' in *Zeitschrift für Kirchengeschichte* 70 (1959) 7; and see G. Theissen *Biblischer Glaube in evolutionärer Sicht* (Munich 1984) pp. 86ff.

3. K. Rahner 'Was ist Häresie?' in *Schriften zur Theologie* V, (Einsiedeln, Zürich, Cologne 1962) pp. 529–530.

4. D. Bonhoeffer *Nachfolge* (Munich 1964) p. 35.

5. E. Schillebeeckx *Jesus* (Freiburg-im-Breisgau 1975) p. 346 (German translation of *Jezus: het verhaal van een levende,* Bloemendaal, 1974).

6. E. Käsemann *Exegetische Versuche und Besinnungen* (Göttingen 1964 pp. 239ff.); *eiusdem Der Ruf der Freiheit* (Tübingen³ 1968) pp. 114ff.; H. Schlier *Die Zeit der Kirche* (Freiburg-im-Breisgau 1955).

7. R. Bultmann *Das Evangelium des Johannes* (Göttingen 1962).

8. E. Käsemann *Jesu letzter Wille nach Joh. 17* (Tübingen 1966) pp. 100ff.

9. G. E. Lessing *Über den Beweis des Geistes und der Kraft* (Zürich 1965 edition of his works, vol. 6, pp. 283ff.).

10. G. E. Lessing *Das Testament Johannis,* in the series cited in note 9, pp. 289ff.

11. P. L. Berger *Der Zwang zur Häresie* (Frankfurt 1980).

12. G. Picht *Wahrheit, Vernunft, Verantwortung* (Stuttgart 1969) pp. 135ff.

13. J. B. Metz *Glaube in Geschichte und Gesellschaft* (Mainz 1977) pp. 3–74.

14. L. Goldmann *Der christliche Bürger und die Aufklärung* (Neuwied 1968).

15. J. B. Metz 'Unterwegs zu einer nachidealistischen Theologie' in *Entwürfe der Theologie,* ed. J. B. Bauer (Graz 1985) p. 214.

16. H. Peukert *Wissenschaftstheorie—Handlungstheorie—Fundamentale Theologie* (Düsseldorf 1976) pp. 280ff.

17. W. Benjamin; see H. Peukert, the work cited in note 16, pp. 278–279.

18. D. Bonhoeffer *Nachfolge,* the edition cited in note 4, at p. 105.

19. D. Bonhoeffer *Widerstand und Ergebung,* new edition (Munich 1970) p. 328.

20. K. Rahner, the article cited in note 3, pp. 554–576.

21. *Theologie aus der Praxis des Volkes* ed. F. Castillo (Munich, Mainz 1978).

Giuseppe Alberigo

Institutional Defence of Orthodoxy

THE PROBLEM of orthodoxy is a permanent one in the life of Christianity, and one that has often brought conflict and damage to the life of the Church. This is why it is important to understand the *different ways in which orthodoxy itself has been understood* and how it has been defended in various historical periods and cultural areas.

Christians were themselves originally objects of accusations of heterodoxy with regard to the ruling religious system of the Roman empire and suffered the consequences of this, including persecution and martyrdom. Because of this, but also due to their need to distance themselves from Judaic orthodoxy, the first generations of Christians proclaimed freedom of conscience and claimed freedom to worship in their own way, rejecting any form of religious restriction.

It was not long, however, before the Christian communities were themselves torn by internal dissent, which took on major doctrinal implications, with damaging results. Donatists, Manichees and Arians raised the problem of the limits of what could be considered authentic apostolic teaching, that is of a *regula fidei*, sharing which became the criterion for true belonging to the Church. In these first centuries, the various churches, markedly divergent from one another as a result of their cultural setting, their derivation from one apostle or another and their very varied internal structures, provided for the defence of orthodoxy through strengthening their communion with each other. This was also expressed through the elaboration of various reference points which, in a non-arbitrary way, served to decide the limits of orthodoxy. The formulations of baptismal symbols, credal professions and agreement on what constituted the canon of the New Testament all belong to this spontaneous process.

The dynamic of this communion between the churches soon found the councils, but also the usual exchanges (such as 'letters of communion') between different communities, to be *important vehicles for verifying orthodoxy*, mutual correction and strengthening in the faith of the apostles and their teaching (*didaché*). With the *ending of the apostolic era* and the radical change in the attitude of the Roman empire in its approach to Christianity, which it first tolerated and then made the official religion, there came important changes in many aspects of the notion and the life of the Church, including the social significance of Christian orthodoxy and the ways in which it should be protected. To the extent that peace within the church had become a decisive factor in the maintenance of good order within the empire, and the good faith of the emperor the guarantee of the purity of orthodoxy, heresy came to be equated with *lèse-majesté*, with the result that persecution of heretics was entrusted to the judicial and police authorities of the empire itself.

Defence of orthodoxy often revolved more around heretical Christians than pagans or Jews, so becoming an internal factor of Christianity rather than an instrument of proselytisation or missionary expansion. This state of affairs was, however, to undergo a sharp reversal, at least in the West, with the fall of the empire and the resultant contacts with the barbarians, events which forced Christianity into a *new period of dynamism*, opening up a great new period of missionary endeavour, in which the dominant concept of faith was as conversion and change of life, rather than adherence to doctrinal statements. It is not without significance that the arena of theological conflict shifted increasingly to the East, where in fact the great councils—Nicea, Constantinople, Ephesus—that gave the Church its basic professions of faith took place.

In these centuries the question of orthodoxy was not set aside, but found institutional expression in councils and synods, which often took on a judiciary function, particularly in regulating relations between bishops and their status in relation to the bishop of Rome. In other words, *pastoral responsibilities included and determined doctrinal ones*, which had no spokesmen or institutions of their own.[1]

This situation changed at the *end of the first millenium of Christianity* as a result of the stabilization of Western European society, which entered its phase of 'Christendom', characterised by a relationship between faith and social community, and between Christianity and society, in which the former made up the basis and inspiration of the latter, which had the duty (and the power) to safeguard the faith. In this context, the way in which faith and the church were understood underwent a profound change, particularly in the way faith was formulated and the institutional ordering of the Church brought about. The development from the *wisdom theology of the patristic period to the scholastic theology of the mendicant orders and the universities* led to an organic formulation of truth, bringing in elements foreign to the credal statements of the early church, thereby enlarging the scope of and multiplying occasions for doctrinal conflict. In turn, the concept of the Church as something increasingly autonomous from biblical theology and Christology accentuated its juridical-institutional aspects, with particular emphasis placed on the role and prerogatives of the church and bishop of Rome. The *reintroduction of Roman law*, along with the birth of a system of law special to the Church alone, were the final elements in forming the context in which the safeguarding of orthodoxy and the struggle against heresy took on increased importance.

Towards the end of the twelfth century the see of Rome concerned itself with establishing *ecclesiastical tribunals dedicated to the fight against heresy*.[2] This was a very significant, though still sporadic, innovation. What it meant was that the defence of orthodoxy was being entrusted to an *ad hoc* Church institution distinct from and increasingly independent of the bishops and their pastoral responsibility. Furthermore, this was to be a judicial institution—a permanent tribunal—something previously unknown, which placed the safeguarding of orthodoxy in an essentially juridical and penal setting, distancing it from the economy of communion (*ex-communicatio*) and the other sacraments and therefore even from the practice of penance and reconciliation of earlier centuries.[3] So the *Inquisition* was born, entrusted mainly to the Order of Preachers and endowed with ever-increasing powers and ever more drastic instruments, including torture and the death penalty. In the late middle ages in the West, the tribunals of the Inquisition became the standard-bearers of Christianity in so far as they pursued the struggle and invoked the sanctions against manifestations of doctrinal (and ideological) deformations, thereby guaranteeing the solidarity of Christian society. Heresy was seen as the primary instrument of the destruction of society; so the 'secular arm' was entrusted with executing the sentences pronounced by the tribunals of the Inquisition.

The request by the king and queen of Spain, towards the end of the fifteenth century, for the establishment of a *State Inquisition*, designed to promote the greater homogeneity of their recently-united kingdom, is an unequivocal illustration of the unique double face of the Inquisition, spiritual and temporal at the same time. We know that Pope Sixtus IV acceded to their request; so was born a tribunal with a sorry reputation for violence, to the degree that even an integrist bishop such as Charles Borromeo opposed its introduction into the State of Milan when this was under Spanish rule.[4]

The tribunals of the Church inquisition underwent a change following *the spread of Lutheranism*. 1542 saw the establishment of the Roman Inquisition by Pope Paul III through the Bull *Licet ab initio* of 21 July. The existing network of tribunals was radically restructured to carry out the struggle against Protestantism through the centralisation of their policy-making and decision-making bodies in Rome, for which it was proposed to set up a cardinalatial Commission. A few years later Paul IV had a list of heretical or presumed-heretical books drawn up; it was forbidden to spread or read these works, under pain of referral to the inquisition tribunals. So the *Index librorum prohibitorum* came into being.

The Inquisition very soon acquired *enormous power*, based not only on its use of drastic and indiscriminate measures (secret delation, refusal of defence to the accused, torture), but also on the complete autonomy of the inquisitorial apparatus, which resisted intervention even from the pope himself. This explains the many voices raised at *Trent in spring 1562*, demanding that those accused should have the right to be heard, that defence could be made against the charges and reconciliation made possible. Likewise, a revision of the Index of forbidden books was called for.[5] After the end of the council, Pius IV did introduce some reforms into the Inquisition and entrusted the revision of the Index to a commission. Then the great reform of the Roman Curia decreed by Sixtus V in 1588 formalised the existence of two Congregations: that of the Holy Inquisition and that of the Index. But resistance to Protestantism prevented any calm reconsideration of the problems relating to the safeguarding of orthodoxy. The churches born of the Reformation were, it must be said, equally intransigent in their approach.

In fact, particularly with the coming of the seventeenth century, the opposition between Catholics and Protestants became stabilised virtually everywhere and the attention of both the Inquisition and the Index were increasingly concentrated on social anomalies (such as witches) or on controversies internal to Catholicism (such as Jansenism). This demonstrated a new shift in the way of looking at faith and the Church. The formulation of faith tended to become fuller and more analytical, less susceptible to variations and differentiations. Scholasticism, after its great period of creativity, was tempted to respond to new problems through immobilism and repetition; contact with the ancient tradition and its sources was increasingly diminished; appeal to the Bible was considered a sign of Protestantism by definition. The Church felt hard pressed by heresies and modern culture and so developed an image of itself as a *besieged citadel*. Just as every yard of a fortress wall is assiduously defended, so every proposition and detail of Catholicism became equally essential and to be defended at whatever cost; in the end, the enemy within became more dangerous than the enemy without.

One factor that served as a moderating influence in this hegemony of 'defence' was the *pastoral dimension of the Tridentine reforms*, shown typically in Benedict XIV's 1753 intervention to make the procedure for condemning books less harsh. But the essential juridical and penal nature of the safeguarding of orthodoxy, and its exercise through a structure parallel to and independent of the churches and their bishops remained intact. A high degree of doctrinal authority was still reserved to the universities, but this was destined to diminish because of the Gallican tendencies of some—notably the Sorbonne—and the growing gap between secular and ecclesiastical culture.

A new turn was introduced by the *French revolution* and the solidarity of the Catholic Church with the *ancien régime* at first and then with the restoration of the monarchy. The pontificate of Gregory XVI was particularly important in this respect; during it the Catholic Church came out of the post-revolutionary turmoil and drew breath once more, finding itself a place in the *Europe of the Restoration and bourgeois hegemony*, a place that meant sharing, though not unconditionally, the features that characterised the new society. This meant that in the first half of the nineteenth century, the Church shared the desire to re-establish a social order whose dominant values were enshrined in an authority that, stripped of the charisms and paternalism of the old order, sought a juridical framework and effective means to assure the new classes of tranquil enjoyment of their new-found hegemony and unlimited exercise of the privileges they had won.

In his programmatic encyclical *Mirari vos*, Gregory XVI set out *lucid criteria for the exercise of papal authority*, criteria that were to guide the basic direction taken by the papacy for the next century and a half. After recalling the risks facing the Church in the 'broad spectrum of evils', and thanking God for allowing it 'a respite from terror', he does not hesitate to say—even if with great distress—that the Church must set aside the '*indulgentiam benignitatis*' and, by virtue of the divine authority it has received, '*virga compescere*'. The encyclical makes specific reference to 1 Cor. 4:21: 'Do I come with a stick in my hand, or in a spirit of love and goodwill?'. This declaration took the papacy completely out of the period of *cura animarum*, setting its understanding of authority on the same level as that found throughout Europe. Mercy seemed to have departed from the public face of Catholicism.

In this way the papacy hastened to give *increasing attention to the doctrinal dimension of the life of the Church*, concerning itself not only with the deposit of faith and the heresies that threatened it, but also with the details of the way the faith was formulated. This corresponded to a diminution in the genres of 'witness' or 'profession' of faith and a more habitual use of the 'teaching' mode, typical of a society very conscious of 'scholarship'. The specific use of the distinction between *ecclesia docens* and *ecclesia discens*, identifying the former with the hierarchy and the latter with the faithful, derives from the same way of thinking.[6]

Pius IX in his turn, with the letter *Tuas libenter* of 1863, not only confirmed the 'proper and original right of ecclesiastical authority to watch over and direct theological doctrine', but also supported the opinion that held that 'faith and obedience should be given only to dogmas expressedly defined by the Church'. So the act of divine faith was extended to theological truths taught by the ordinary *magisterium* of the bishops not necessarily meeting in council, and even to doctrinal decisions made by the Roman congregations. There was an excessive extension of the scope of doctrinal decisions binding in faith, and therefore of the areas of control of the Holy Inquisition and the Congregation for the Index. This was a significant indication of the fact that for several decades the papacy and the Roman congregations had been effecting a shift of the epicentre of the Church's governing actions *from the sphere of discipline to that of doctrine*. Responsibility for doctrine was withdrawn from the authority of synods, where it had previously resided, and concentrated in mainly bureaucratic and administrative bodies set up for carrying out government directives and not for safeguarding orthodoxy. Doctrinal polycentrism, which for centuries had nourished a balanced and fruitful dynamism from respect for the conclusive value of the *sensus fidei* expressed through the *congregatio fidelium*, was completely eclipsed.

The *dominant ecclesiology of Vatican I*, presupposing the lowly and passive position of the faithful, allowed authority to put forward even more definite interventions in the fluid sphere of doctrine. All the more so in that, accepting and perhaps enduring the challenge of lay philosophy, the ecclesiastical *magisterium* insisted almost exclusively on *abstract and de-historicised acceptance of formulations of faith*, presenting revelation as a truth abstracted from the historical process and destined by its nature to be imparted from above. A ready-made truth, placed at the tip of the triangle, with regard to which the only reactions could be full acceptance or error. So the council consolidated the tendencies of the post-revolutionary period: a generally repressive effort by doctrinal authorities and their concentration at the apex of the ecclesiastical triangle, and whose pronouncements would all receive the maximum formal acceptance.

In relation to this tendency, Newman's insistence on the undeniable value of the *sensus fidelium* as the determinant factor in establishing the fidelity of the Church to revelation took on special importance. He refused to accept that the consent of the faithful was implicit in decisions made by the 'teaching Church'; if that had been the case, he remarked, the Church would on some occasions have fainted away at orthodoxy.

At the start of the present century, the *modernist controversy* dramatically accentuated this whole problem. Pius X, who changed the name of the Congregation for the Inquisition to the Congregation of the Holy Office, in

1907 authorised the publication of a decree which condemned more than sixty theological propositions, followed by that of the encyclical *Pascendi*, which turned the doubts of the modernists into a complete doctrinal system in order to refute it in its entirety. It is worth noting that the long list of errors proscribed in the decree *Lamentabili* began with a group of theses relating to the authority of the ecclesiastical *magisterium*, including the Roman congregations. The anti-modernist campaign thereby introduced another novel element, the rabidness with which errors and those in error were pursued, something not seen since the harshest phases of anti-Protestant persecutions. A *whole system sprang up*: delations, secret and arbitrary trials, a search for coercive measures such as ruining individuals in every possible way. Mercy and reconciliation seemed to be feared and rejected, replaced with obedience alone and complete submission to the truth and its fearful custodians.

It would be a mistake to believe that people in Rome behaved like this because of moral barbarism; it was rather the *development of a basic orientation in line with the shift of the axis of Church government into the doctrinal sphere*, using the delicate and sensitive instrument of discernment of doctrinal conformity to the Gospel as a daily tool for regulating the life of the church community. When Pius X, in 1913, declared that the renewed Congregation of the Holy Office was to have the additional title 'supreme', besides being the only one presided over by the pope, this gave institutional sanction to a complex process of evolution. The Catholic Church, on the eve of the dramatic explosion of the 'ideological' phase of European society, furnished itself with a strongly centralised bureaucratic organ devoted, with no outside control save that of the final responsibility of the pope, to seeking out and condemning error. An enviable anticipation of the ideological States, or a tragic step on the way of radical reduction of pluralism and suppression of all minorities under pretext of error? Given that the times favoured specialist authorities, was it not a responsible act to entrust the defence of doctrine in matters of faith and customs, as canon 246 of the new *Codex iuris canonici* of 1917 put it, to a highly specialised organ? The fact that this very act deprived the church as *universitas fidelium* and even the hierarchy itself of this responsibility was to become clear only with time.

The third and fourth decades of the twentieth century were thus to mark the apogee of the effective power exercised by the Holy Office over the Church. Suffice to recall its interventions in matters of ecumenical dialogue, ecclesial and theological renewal and then Catholic-Marxist dialogue, to see how all the crucial problems facing Catholicism at this time were subjected to control by the supreme authority through doctrinal intervention. This approach reached its height with Pius XII's encyclical *Humani Generis* in 1950. In this, he rejected the insights that had been developed, mainly in France under the general title of '*théologie nouvelle*', and produced a sort of 'magna carta' of the previous century's line on doctrinal authority.

The enormous upheaval produced by the second world war left the world divided into two opposing camps, starting a period of acute ideological confrontation. But it has been a period in which *instruments of power have not triumphed, but rather gone into decline*. A slow decline, and an uneven one, which has raised new and worrying questions about the concept and specific exercise of power in all societies. The *second Vatican Council* opened in 1962, at the hesitant dawn of all this. The opening session on 11 October was one of the highlights of the whole council thanks to the way John XXIII's opening discourse set the tone and the programme for the council. He expressed the hope that the council would be in line with the teaching of the Church and would represent this to all people in a manner that took account of the failings, demands and opportunities of our times. The speech went on to make a crucial point: the assessment of the historical moment in which the council had assembled. The pope held that 'the present order of things' was characterised by 'a new order of human relations' not seen before. Backing this assessment up with a hermeneutical criterion, the pope reproved—with unusual harshness—those who saw 'in these modern times ... nothing but prevarication and ruin', those who say that 'our era, in comparison with past eras, is getting worse'. And he declared solemnly: 'We feel we must disagree with those prophets of doom.'

Pope John went on to say: 'the substance of the ancient doctrine of the deposit of faith is one thing, and the way in which it is presented is another', thereby recalling the Church to a true understanding of the substantial difference between divine revelation and ecclesiastical definitions. But the heart of the Catholic *magisterium* had for over a century been fixed on the struggle against error, as proclaimed by Gregory XVI. On the eve of Vatican II, John XXIII also put the thorny problem of how to exercise doctrinal authority into historical perspective. The Church has 'frequently condemned (errors) with the greatest severity. Nowadays, however, the Spouse of Christ prefers to make use of the medicine of mercy rather than that of severity. She considers that she meets the needs of the present day by demonstrating the validity of her teaching rather than by condemnations.'[7] So, exactly 130 years later, another successor of Peter proclaimed an approach diametrically opposed to that of 1832, taking account of the maturing evangelical understanding of the Church and of the changed historical circumstances.

We know that Vatican II made definite changes to the hierarchical and authoritarian outlook of contemporary Catholicism, putting forward a *criterion of communion as the measure for the life of the Church* in all its aspects.

Many council Fathers stressed the need for the Church to find a new style based on mercy. But it is equally clear that there is an undeniable divergence between the pointers given by John XXIII and the conclusions reached in the conciliar documents, a divergence which has had a considerable impact on the post-conciliar Church, often depriving it of clear, broad and unequivocal motivation and direction.

In accordance with the clearly voted wishes of the council, *Paul VI*, on the day the council closed, *restructured the Holy Office* through the *motu proprio Integrae servandae*, as a forerunner to a general reform of the Roman curia. His premises expressed in the *motu proprio* re-echoed some of the motives dear to John XXIII, particularly the need to take account of historical changes and abandon a mainly repressive approach. 'Since charity casts out fear,' he wrote 'the defence of faith is *now* better served by promoting doctrine ...'. Because of this approach the Holy Office was not abolished completely but—taking up a suggestion originally made by De Lai in 1907—was re-named the Congregation 'for the Doctrine of the Faith', lost its title of 'supreme' and underwent a series of modifications, before having its functions regulated, something that had never been done till that moment, so as to emphasise the completely discretionary nature of this organ.

In June 1966 the Index of forbidden books was declared no longer canonically valid.[8] At the beginning of the following year the Congregation for the Doctrine of the Faith asked all the episcopal conferences to set up their own doctrinal commissions, an initiative which established a network linked to the Congregation itself, but at the same time had the effect of linking it to pastoral organs such as the conferences. The general reform of the curia in August 1967 laid down norms for the operation of the Congregation for the Doctrine of the Faith, also providing for it to be linked to the Pontifical Biblical Commission and a new international theological Commission.[9]

Finally, in early 1971, there appeared the long-awaited *Nova agenda ratio*, regulating proceedings instituted by the Congregation itself.[10] The *Ratio*, while providing some embryonic safeguards for the rights of those being examined, still left open the basic problem of the nature—administrative or penal—of the proceedings themselves, a problem fraught with consequences due to the effects the pronouncements of the Congregation can have.[11]

The initiatives taken by the Congregation over the past few years show that the post-conciliar reform—which went way beyond the suggestions made by those responsible for the Congregation—was seriously inadequate. *Ecclesiologically inadequate*, in that it deputes questions of safeguarding orthodoxy to a body distinct from and isolated from the people of God and from those responsible for pastoral care; *theologically inadequate*, in that it makes reference to an abstract and ideologised acceptance of the deposit of faith to the detriment of its pastoral nature and multiform riches; *historically inadequate*, because it is still strictly bound to models of ideological conformism which the modern world has superseded. To the extent that all this is. true, it follows that orthodoxy and its defence are, despite their importance, being placed in the false light of an approach that is both obsolete and contradictory to the ends it is supposed to serve, thereby inflicting unacceptable damage on both.

Translated by Paul Burns

Notes

1. See R. Eno 'Preservation and Interpretation: the Church of the Fathers' in *Concilium* 12 (1976/7) and C. Vogel 'Penance and Excommunication in the Early Church and during the High Middle Ages' in *Concilium* 11 (1975/7).

2. See H. Maisonneuve *Etudes sur les origines de l'Inquisition* (Paris 1942); K. Pennington '*Pro peccatis patrum puniri?* A moral and legal problem of the Inquisition' in *Church History* 47 (1978) 137–154; E. van der Vekene '*Bibliotheca bibliographica historiae sanctae Inquisitionis*' in *Bibliographisches Verzeichnis des gedruckten Schrifttums zur Geschichte und Literatur der Inquisition* (Vaduz 1983, 2 vols.).

3. For the growth of a concept of *iurisdictio* separate from the sacramental dimension of *ordo* in the twelfth century, see B. Tierney *Religion, Law and the Growth of Constitutional Thought, 1150–1650* (Cambridge 1982) p. 30.

4. Among the most recent studies are: *La Inquisición española. Nueva visión, nuevos horizontes* ed. J. Pérez Villaneuva (Madrid 1980); V. Pinto Crespo *Inquisición y control ideológico en la España del siglo XVI* (Madrid 1983); *Inquisición española y mentalided inquisitoria* ed. A. Alcalá (Barcelona 1954).

5. H. Jedin *The History of the Council of Trent* (IV, 1).

6. This section summarizes my analysis in 'The Authority of the Church in the Documents of Vatican I and Vatican II' in *Journal of Ecumenical Studies* 19 (1982) 119–145.

7. The full text of the speech is in *The Documents of Vatican II* ed. W. Abbott (London-Dublin 1966) pp. 710–719.

8. '*Post apostolicas litteras*' in AAS 58 (1966). In 1917 Benedict XV had merged the Congregation for the Index with that of the Holy Office.

9. Cf. S. Alvárez Menéndez 'La reforma de la Congregación del Santo Oficio' in *Revista española de derecho canónico* 21 (1966); for a more general study see my 'Serving the Communion of Churches' in *Concilium* 15 (1979/7).

10. AAS 63 (1971) pp. 234–236. See A. Alcaina Canosa '*Nova agendi ratio in doctrinarum examine*' in *Rev. esp. de der. can.* 28 (1972).

11. The new Code of Canon Law has left out all the canons relating to the Roman congregations and as a result the Congregation for the Doctrine of the Faith is mentioned only in can. 1362, 1, dealing with offences reserved to its competence, of which there is no mention in any other canon in the same Code!

Iring Fetscher

Orthodoxy and Heresy in Marxism-Leninism and Psycho-Analysis

DOXA, AS everyone knows, means 'opinion'. Since opinions are subjective, there can be only one rule for their co-existence, *tolerance*. Marx's theory, however, claims to be a science. Scientific knowledge advances by the correction of errors and the emergence of new paradigms which have greater plausibility than the earlier ones, which does not imply that previous conclusions were necessarily 'wrong'. Marx himself once said that his favourite motto was *De omnibus dubitandum*. This was the path to knowledge pioneered by René Descartes, in opposition to the older philosophy, which relied on authorities. In science there can only ever be 'temporary' and questionable authorities, never permanent ones. Accordingly, as long as Marx's theory was represented by a multiplicity of authors teaching, writing and discussing alongside each other, without any authoritative institution with power to define the theory, *the theory developed*, even if not every contribution to it advanced knowledge.

Even in the *young Soviet Union*, a lively academic dispute arose shortly after 1917 between Marxists more heavily influenced by Hegel and his dialectic and Marxists who followed a positivist idea of science. At first it made *no sense to talk of orthodoxy and heresy*. It is true that Lenin was convinced of the correctness of his own interpretation of Marxism, and fought 'deviant' opinions with extreme severity, but these 'deviants' were not yet heretics as long as there was no institution which claimed the authority to issue infallible interpretations against which there was no appeal. This happened first in the *Stalin period*. Whereas there had been only a small number of basic 'guidelines' for thought (and action), such as the primacy of matter over consciousness, the forward movement of historical development, the superiority of socialism to capitalism, more and more propositions were now decreed to be 'unshakable dogmas' of Marxism-Leninism (which was an invention of Stalin's).

The result of this *dogmatisation of theory*, its transformation into a sort of doctrine, was that, in every conceivable area of scholarship and research, advances in knowledge were not only not assisted, but directly prevented. The most blatant example was the field of genetics, where *Lysenko's 'theories'*, apparently the only theories compatible with an orthodox dialectical materialism, triumphed over 'Morganism' when the political leadership 'decreed' that genetics was a 'reactionary and imperialist' doctrine incompatible with Marxism-Leninism. The result of this decree was wrong investments in agriculture (afforestation was based on Lysenko's views) and the neglect of genetic research, so that the development of new varieties lagged behind that of Western countries. Much the same attitude was adopted by Soviet scientific bureaucrats to Einstein's theory of relativity. The crucial role of the theory for research and theory construction in physics was recognised only late in the day, after it had proved possible to 'reconcile' this theory with orthodoxy by 'reinterpreting' it.

In 1955, in his essay 'Current and non-current concepts in Marxism', Leszek Kolakowski distinguished between an *'intellectual'* and an *'institutional'* Marxism. It was only this institutional Marxism which makes it possible to talk of *orthodoxy and heresy*. Among the characteristics of this conception were the requirement that a person 'should profess adherence to Marxism-Leninism', as if it were possible to 'profess adherence' to a scientific theory (which is what Marxism claims to be), and the fact that the utterances of the competent authority—the Central Committee of the Communist Party of the Soviet Union or the general secretary of the party—have to be 'believed'. However, the contents of this belief are not fixed once and for all, but are varied by the same institution according to need and circumstance. Kolakowski writes:

The true Marxist professes adherence to views the content of which he has no need to understand. As every Marxist in 1950 knew, Lysenko's inheritance theory was correct, Hegel's philosophy was an aristocratic reaction to the French Revolution, Dostoyevsky was a 'corrupt decadent' and Babayevsky an outstanding writer.[1] Ssuvorov was a champion of progress and the resonance theory in chemistry outdated rubbish. Every Marxist knew this even if he or she had never heard of chromosomes, didn't know what century Hegel had lived in, hadn't read a single short story of Dostoyevsky's or never read a secondary school chemistry textbook. A

Marxist did not need to bother with all that, since the content of Marxism was fixed by the authorities.[2]

Kolakowski compares this process of fixing the 'orthodox' content of 'doctrine' with *'Church doctrine'*. The crucial difference is that Marxism-Leninism at the same time makes *a claim to be a science*, and the establishment of 'orthodox' views and the rejection of 'heretical' ones is incompatible with science.

> There can (indeed) be dispute about whether a theory meets the criteria of scientific thought better or worse, and these criteria also include—but not exclusively—the main rules of the method developed by Marx. But these rules have to be fairly general, and they do not contain any detailed instructions regarding the assessment of this or that historical phenomenon. They always allow a number of interpretations. The rule of historical materialism as such in no case prescribes the intensity or the degree of clarity with which the material conditions of life influence human social thought in any particular historical period. Nor does it insist in advance, for example, that Pascal's philosophy is an expression of the fall of the feudal aristocracy which was deprived of its influence or the embodiment of bourgeois thought, or anything else. In sociological, and still more in philosophical, investigations there is not one absolutely unambiguous concept, and this instability in terminology is transferred to all tenets of the doctrine, however fundamental they may be, none of which can be described as unambiguous.[3]

Kolakowski comes to the illuminating conclusion that whatever is scientifically useful in Marx's views has gradually been, or will be, absorbed by the general methodology of the historical and social sciences, while any other doctrines must be regarded as ideology and so as unscientific. So 'the most important division ... is no longer between orthodox Marxists—whose main aim is to protect the purity of their doctrine from pagan influences—and all others', but between *a 'humanistic left and a humanistic right'*.[4] The label 'Marxism', Kolakowski says, will itself disappear to the extent that its scientifically tenable insights are absorbed by science. This process naturally takes place more slowly in the human sciences than in the natural sciences, and in a different way.[5]

The special paradox of the transformation of Marx's critical theory, which considers itself a science, into a doctrine whose 'purity' is watched over by a specially authorised agency is sharply highlighted by a comparison with Marx's conception of *ideology*. According to Marx, ideologies are restrictions on perception resulting from the blindness of individuals because of interests stemming from their class affiliation. This proven critique of 'false consciousness' is itself called in question by the hypothesis that the perspective of the proletariat makes possible for the first time an understanding of history and society which is free of ideology, and that the communist party, as the 'embodiment' of 'the proletariat's correct class consciousness' is the only legitimate 'possessor' of this ideology-free knowledge.

Kolakowski sums up this *development from Mark through Lenin to doctrinaire Leninism* as follows:

> The peculiar and historically unique antinomy in the evolution of Marxism consists in the fact that this doctrine which [originally] exposed the way social consciousness is mystified under the pressure of political conditions, and proclaimed its total liberation from myth, has itself fallen victim to such a mystification.[6]

The theoretical defect which made this development possible even in Marx was the implication that ownership of the means of production and the reification of social relations under capitalism were the only factors which could produce false consciousness. In this connection Kolakowski speaks generally of 'political conditions', where Marx and the Marxists saw only the social conditions of a class society as capable of distorting knowledge and behaviour; Marx did not see forsee the possibility that the interests of a bureaucratic institution such as the communist party (and the whole 'nomenklatura class') could also have such an effect. He probably did not envisage this because he had naive ideas of the 'political form' of the 'transitional society' between capitalism and socialism and believed in the possibility of a form of direct democracy without bureaucracy and without a standing army (but with a police force which could at any time be 'voted out of office'). The long road from Marx's *de omnibus dubitandum* to the idea that the party is always right illustrates the development from a theory which was at least intended as a critical science to a doctrine to be believed as 'orthodox'.

Similar phenomena can be found in scientific theories wherever distinct 'schools' contend publicly for recognition and have to assert themselves against hostile criticism. Another example of this is *Sigmund Freud's psychoanalysis*. For a long time Freud's genuinely epoch-making insights had to face the implacable resistance of the whole of orthodox medicine, and especially of psychiatry. This fact, together with Freud's undeniable authoritarian (and patriarchal) attitude led to a situation in which any member of his 'school' who deviated even in a single crucial point from the founder's theory, now becoming an orthodoxy, was 'expelled' from the community and even declared anathema. This happened in turn with Alfred Adler, with C. G. Jung and finally with Wilhelm Reich, who was in addition 'excommunicated' by Marxist 'orthodoxy'.[7] Even though the effects of these anathemas can in no sense be compared with those faced by 'deviants' or 'heretics' in Marxism-Leninism within the territories controlled by State socialism, the damage done to the development of the theory is fully comparable. A consequence of the need for demarcation was the breaking off of discussion and so—as J. S. Mill predicted—a *restriction of the progress of knowledge*. Analysts like Karen Horney or Erich Fromm in his late period, who supplemented psycho-analysis with ego-theory and cultural criteria, were rejected as 'revisionists' rather than given critical appraisal for their views. 'Deviation' from orthodoxy was often sufficient reason for the rejection of a theoretical innovation. Quite apart from whether the view concerned was important and a development of knowledge or not, the breaking off of communications was a *breach of the principle of 'non-dominative discourse'* which underlies all scientific research. Within such discourse no opinion or view may be given privileged status as 'orthodox', but all must be discussed as having an equal claim to truth.

The end-point of the development of 'orthodoxies' outside the sphere of the churches is always—not by coincidence—a *'doctrine of infallibility'*. For Marxism-Leninism the Communist Party of the Soviet Union was for a long time the 'infallible authority' (which proclaimed 'truths of last instance', as Robert Havemann ironically remarked[8]). For psycho-analysis the authority was Freud in his lifetime, and after his death Anna Freud or the leadership of the Psycho-Analytic Society. Since analysis developed a different character in different cultural and political environments, not surprisingly a number of such associations in the end came into being which condemned each other as being more or less 'heretical'. At the time of the Chinese cultural revolution the ideological split and the political opposition of Soviet and Chinese communists also led to mutual excommunication, that is, to a denial of the other side's right to call itself 'Marxist-Leninist'.

Leszek Kolakowski notes with sociological sobriety that *such behaviour is natural to political organisations*. 'Once created as a social fact, the organisation has at least one interest of its own, to maintain internal cohesion, which requires relentless opposition to any attempt at disruption.' For an artificial organisation—a party or a scientific school whose members support each other to the hilt in the face of a critical or hostile public—'a disruption of consciousness is annihilation, and so it must defend its ideology with every possible means against 'critical questioning'.[9]

Examples from the extra-ecclesial use of the dichotomy orthodox-heterodox show that this demarcation is always the work of organisations whose *interest in self-preservation requires the preservation (and transmission unchanged) of a binding ideology.* Such institutions outwardly behave in an authoritarian manner towards their members, while their posture towards other institutions is defensive. In so far as a new scientific theory is relieved of the need to wage a battle to establish itself, the disputes between 'schools' or 'associations' lose this character and may develop into appropriate forms of scientific discussion. Parties and schools—to the extent that they behave as closed organisations—are harmful to the discovery of truth and the development of scientific knowledge.

Translated by Francis McDonagh

Notes

1. Babayevsky, Sergei, a mediocre Soviet writer and representative of 'Socialist realism'.
2. Leszek Kolakowski, 'Actuelle und nichtaktuelle Begriffe des Marxismus' in *id. Der Mensch ohne Alternative, von der Möglichkeit und Unmöglichkeit Marxist zu sein* (Münich 1960) p. 9.
3. *Ibid.* pp. 19ff.
4. *Ibid.* p. 21.
5. *Ibid.* p. 23.
6. *Ibid.* p. 27.
7. Freud's dispute with Alfred Adler and C. G. Jung is described in Freud's essay 'On the History of the Psycho-Analytic Movement' (S. Freud *Complete Psychological Works*, ed. J. Strachey, XIV, London, 1957). Freud here elaborates on Adler's 'personal motive'. Adler, says Freud, 'announced in the presence of a small circle of members of the Vienna group [the Psycho-Analytical Society] "Do you think it gives me such great pleasure to stand in your shadow my whole life long?" ' Freud comments: 'To be sure, I see nothing reprehensible in a younger man freely admitting his ambition, which one could guess in any case was among the incentives for his work. But even though a man is dominated by a motive of this kind he should know how to avoid being ... "unfair". How little Adler has succeeded in this is shown by the profusion of petty outbursts of malice which disfigure his writings and by the indications they contain of an uncontrolled craving for priority' (p. 51). 'Everything Adler has to say about dreams, the shibboleth of psycho-analysis, is equally empty and unmeaning' (p. 57).
   'Adler's secession (sic) took place before the Weimar Congress in 1911; after that date the Swiss began theirs. The first signs of it, curiously enough, were a few remarks of Riklin's in some popular articles appearing in Swiss publications, so that the general public learned earlier than those intimately concerned in the subject that psycho-analysis had got the better of some regrettable errors which had previously discredited it. In 1912 Jung boasted, in a letter from America, that his modification of psycho-analysis had overcome the resistances of many people who had hitherto refused to have

anything to do with it. I replied that he had nothing to boast of, and that the more he sacrificed of the hard-won truths of psycho-analysis the more he would see resistances vanishing. This modification which the Swiss were so proud of introducing was again nothing else but a pushing into the background of the sex factor in psycho-analytic theory. I confess that from the beginning I regarded this "advance" as too far-reaching an adjustment to the demands of actuality' (p. 58).

'His approach to the standpoint of the masses, his abandonment of an innovation which proved unwelcome, make it *a priori* improbable that Jung's corrected version of psycho-analysis can justly claim to be a youthful act of liberation. After all, it is not the age of the doer that decides this, but the character of the deed' (pp. 59–60).

'When, after irreconcilable scientific differences had come to light, I was obliged to bring about Adler's resignation from the editorship of the *Zentralblatt*, he left the Vienna society as well, and founded a new one, which at first adopted the tasteful name of 'The Society for Free Psycho-Analysis'. But outsiders who are unconnected with analysis are evidently unskillful in appreciating the differences between two psycho-analysts. ... 'Free' psycho-analysis remained in the shadow of 'official', 'orthodox' psycho-analysis and was treated merely as an appendage to the latter. Then Adler took a step for which we are thankful; he severed all connection with psycho-analysis, and gave his theory the name of "Individual Psychology" ' (pp. 51–52).

8. Robert Havemann *Rückantworten an die Hauptverwaltung 'Ewige Wahrheiten'* (München 1970).

9. Leszek Kolakowski, in the work cited in note 2, at p. 29.

PART III

Practical Aspects

Herbert Vorgrimler

The Adventure of a New 'World Catechism'

THE 'SECOND extraordinary synod' of bishops voted a concluding document on 9 December 1985 which mentions among its specific themes 'the sources of the Church's life'. These sources are the word of God and the liturgy. The heading 'the word of God' covers (1) scripture, tradition and *magisterium*, (2) evangelisation, (3) the relationship between the teaching office of the bishops and theologians. Following from this, under '(4) Recommendations', we find: 'There is a unanimous desire for a catechism or compendium of the whole of Catholic teaching on faith and morals, as a sort of reference point for the catechisms or compendia to be produced in the different regions. The presentation must be biblical and liturgical, it must offer true doctrine and at the same time be adapted to the modern outlook on life of believers'.[1]

The excellent special secretary of this synod, the dogmatic theologian Walter Kasper, reports in his short commentary:

This suggestion did not come from the curia at all; it was not the product of a centralising mentality. It came first from the periphery, from churches of the Third World, though it was then adopted by European and North American bishops too. When the synod, for obvious reasons, did not act on it immediately, it was put forward again by several language groups.[2]

Awareness of this background is important for a critical evaluation; *the new plan does not conceal an attempt at indoctrination into uniformity, but expresses an urgent desire of the 'periphery'*. This desire was not expressed with any defensive intention, and certainly not with the intention of retaining the old

Euro-centrism, but positively and constructively. Walter Kasper points to the connection with the *inculturation of Christianity*, and this alone indicates a rejection of a Euro-centric view. Kasper believes that in this unpredictable and irresistible process of the inculturation of Christianity in the so-called 'Third World', a drifting apart (of local churches, of individual Christians?) in central truths of the faith would be fatal (for the Church?).[3] Clearly we find here the idea that there can be something like a *fixed, unchangeable 'deposit' of teaching of faith and morals* which 'in itself' has never been affected by history and may not be affected by transmission in the processes of inculturation. It is easy to see why this idea is very seductive, since it guarantees firm ground under the feet, in the heads and in the mouths of preachers and teachers in any conceivable situation in which the Church may find itself. However, it is more problematic than is realised or admitted, because it conceives of this 'deposit' on the model of Platonic ideas, and does not allow for essential features of Christianity such as the *history of dogma* and its understanding.

Even if, for the sake of argument, we accept this comforting idea, we still need to ask why we need a new book. Are there not solid printed testimonies which contain this fundamental deposit? Is there not holy scripture, Denzinger-Schönmetzer, along with many catechisms and summaries, from the *Catechismus Romanus* to Paul VI's *Credo of the People of God*? The synod's statement implicitly answers this question.

1. A TASK FOR FUNDAMENTAL THEOLOGY

We shall start from the hypothesis that such a book is desirable and possible.

If we consider the *four principles* laid down by the synod for the production of this book, we find ourselves confronted with the first: The presentation must be *biblically based*. What does it mean to talk about a biblical basis for the whole of the Church's teaching on faith and morals? If this task is tackled seriously—and we have no doubt that the synod wants serious work—the biblical basis cannot consist of some sort of excerpts from holy scripture. Nor can there be an advance statement: 'God has spoken, and he said this.' Such a positivist statement about revelation would not be understood. As a preliminary it would be necessary to clarify what was meant by 'God speaking', by revelation and by hearing and understanding the word of God. This, however, would take us into a complex set of hermeneutical problems, and these would also surface if the starting point were not biblical, but *liturgical or ethical and dogmatic* (points 2 and 3 of the synod's principles).

The hermeneutics such a book would have to offer *belongs to fundamental theology before it is biblical,* and its fundamental task is to relate the actual and possible experiences of God in the present to the memories of God attested in the Church's message. It is true that there are experiences of God which are structurally 'internationalised': the experiences of transcendence possible in knowledge and love, the moral experiences of an absolute obligation of conscience. Nevertheless one may doubt whether they can easily be transmitted in an 'internationalised' language. After all, such statements exist already on an abstract level, as for example in the so-called proofs of the existence of God. The initiation intended in this proposal would have to bundle together particular testimonies of faith from every possible situation in which believers find themselves.

Once this complex and very delicate process has shown what experiences of God Christians are having today, they will have to be exposed to the test of confrontation with the memories embodied in the Jewish and Christian religious tradition. This process will lead to a clarification; it will not simply help to bring us closer to what is 'objectively valid' in modern experiences of God, but will also, through the power of memory, destabilise overly objective, abstract language. Demanding, liberating forces of faith will appear, and impulses to disagreement and opposition, and all backed by polycentric documentation.[4]

What is the point of all this elaboration? The point is that without it it is quite impossible to say what 'use'—to put it crudely and inadequately—faith is. The positivist ideas of revelation so often used today in talking about God, because they are more comfortable, completely fail to show how God can be used, and is indeed necessary—this again is crude and abstract—to protect the mystery of the human person, its unique dignity, from banality and instrumentalisation, and to provide a basis for moral responsibility among human beings without which we are bound to degenerate into absolute barbarism. At the Second Vatican Council the Church asserted that it existed to be 'a sign of and protection for the transcendence of the human person' (*Gaudium et Spes* 76). In other words, this sort of broad theological discussion of the basis of faith and its practice is part of the core of what we have to hold fast.

2. THE SYNOD'S FOUR PRINCIPLES

Only after such preliminaries does it make sense to consider the synod's wish, the provision of a biblical basis for 'the whole of Catholic teaching on faith and morals'. The tasks before us here are no less demanding. The synod cannot have meant simply collecting the biblical 'proofs' from Denzinger-

Schönmetzer. The basis thus provided must be able to stand up to opposition in the process of inculturation; it would be wrong for the Church to 'export' something from which it itself is still suffering. In other words, there is an urgent need, when providing this biblical basis, to *put an end to the two-track approach to biblical and historical truth on the one hand and dogmatic truth on the other*. If this is not done, the Church's proclamation of the faith will not be credible. The authors of the new world catechism ought therefore to heed the ancient and profound maxim: *Quis nimis probat nihil probat* ('To prove too much is to prove nothing').

To give only one example out of many, we must once and for all stop misusing Luke 10:16. The existence and authority of the Church's teaching office cannot be based on this saying ('Whoever hears you hears me'), which is a stock Semitic messenger-commissioning formula, or all ecclesiastical utterances would be like the words of Jesus, infallible. The Church's *moral teaching*, including its social teaching, will create its own special problems. It is clear that there are areas in the field of human culture, ecology, economics, technology and so on, on which the Church has made dogmatic statements, although these areas were not present in biblical revelation. It will be fascinating to see what the biblical basis in these areas looks like.

The synod's call for the new world catechism to have a *liturgical orientation* reflects the new weight given to liturgy in theology[5] and of course, in the wake of the Second Vatican Council and its liturgical reform, in the Church's practice too. This guideline would be most valuable if *Catholic teaching on faith and morals were consistently fitted into the great doxological dynamic of the Church*. How wonderful it would be to have a moral teaching not obsessed with a few difficult areas and exhausting itself in rigid stereotypes—this must be one reason for the Church's disastrous lack of authority among ordinary Catholics—but which would, without liberalism, proclaim the freedom for which God's children have been set free and lead to the glory of God.

Nonetheless even liturgy is not without its problems, and in the production of such a distinguished book they would have to be recognised and, as far as possible, dealt with. It cannot be assumed that a liturgical orientation in this case means that the whole task of a polycentric inculturation and 'indigenisation' in the field of liturgy can be achieved with one book. Should it then deal only with what in the liturgy must everywhere be identical because— for example—it has to do with the 'validity' of the sacraments? There are *similar fundamental questions here* as in the case of the biblical basis. There will be a need for a new sensibility to the *language* in which the relevant topics are expressed. We will have to consider whether it is at all possible to talk about the Church's '*powers*' without doing violence to the absolute and sacred sovereignty of God, which cannot be controlled by liturgical ministers. We will have to pay much more attention to liturgy as *petition* (*epiclesis*) in order to avoid any appearance of magic or an automatic mechanism, particularly in attempts at inculturation. There is a practical question too. Surely the universally valid liturgical rules, the narrow perspective of conditions and validity, powers and the empowered, are already contained in the new code of canon law? Does this not create the danger that, for liturgy too, a universally valid catechism might become a summary of a summary?

The synod's *third principle* says that the new world catechism should offer the '*correct doctrine*' (*Walter Kasper says the 'sound' doctrine*)[6] *of the Church.* If all that was involved were the distinction between what is the teaching of the Church as proclaimed or recognised by the full authority of the extraordinary and ordinary *magisterium* of the Church and legitimately expressed theological hypotheses, interpretations, attempts at clarification and the like, the task would be as easy as it would be superfluous. All that would be needed would be to pick up Denzinger-Schönmetzer and other respectable compendia of the Church's official teaching, and the people responsible for inculturation would do the updating.

Is it, however, so easy? The Church's official teaching is an enormously complex structure, in part derived over almost two millennia merely from *historically conditioned controversies and in part in urgent need of interpretation.* Research into the history of dogma has shown that much which is described in manuals as 'dogma' is not in fact dogma, but a venerable practice of the Church once protected by a conciliar anathema. Who is to decide whether such a statement or a practice protected in this way still deserves protection? They may even no longer exist, and if so will they be taken to the Third World for inculturation? The 'sound doctrine' once proclaimed with such investment of authority includes a good deal which is only of interest to the question of a previous age. Is the new world catechism to give answers to yesterday's questions, which no-one is asking any more? This third principle presupposes a complete examination of the corpus of doctrine with the use of precise criteria from the history of dogma and the human sciences. And what is to happen to 'unsound' or incorrect teaching? If the new book is to offer only sound doctrine, who will protect the so-called 'Third World' from unsound doctrine? After all, it is not immediately recognisable as unsound. Or is the new world catechism an opportunity to deal with undesirable theological views? Question after question, task after task.

Following the three principles already mentioned may seem complicated, but the real difficulties only begin with the *fourth principle.* The presentation must be '*adapted to the modern outlook on life of the faithful*', the synod says. This principle is not in itself intelligible and acceptable. There are at least *three reasons for questioning it.*

First, there is *no such thing as 'the modern outlook on life'*; such an expression is extremely trivial. What it refers to is nothing other than the extremely divergent situations and mentalities in the so-called Third World, but the new world catechism cannot itself perform the task of inculturation it is intended to support. Second, there is *no universal language* for 'the modern outlook on life'.[7] Presumably the idea is not that this language is Latin. If so, then Denzinger-Schönmetzer and the new code of canon law would be all we need. Third, the word 'adapted' is of course well-intentioned, but much more *dangerous* than the synod fathers realised. Anyone who holds on to belief in the divine origin of the Church's message can only tirelessly—hoping against hope—work to adapt the world to the gospel and not vice versa. There are so many, such overlapping *resistances* on the part of the divine message to this world and its perspectives that it is essentially impossible to adapt. The result is that the puzzled reader of this appeal is left merely with the assumption that it proclaims the intention to keep the new volume free from outmoded views of the world and the thinking associated with them—out of respect for genuine scholasticism I prefer not to talk about 'scholastic' thinking.

This, however, is a task which is larger and more difficult than can be lightly demanded.

3. IS EUROPE EXPORTING THE ENLIGHTENMENT?

Christians' interpretations of the world are always also ideas of God. If an 'unmodern' picture of the world ('attitude to life') falls into disuse, a particular image of God falls with it. But this means nothing other than the transfer of the process of the European Enlightenment into the regions of the so-called 'Third World'. The main source of the unencumbered freshness, the fascinating naivety and the strength of these people's faith is the fact that the issues of the Enlightenment have so far not penetrated to them. The examples could fill a whole book, but simply consider the miraculous interventions into this-worldly reality attributed to the Virgin of Guadelupe or the Virgin of Czestochowa. The Enlightenment is a process which on the whole is unavoidable, and wearily reflects the faith of old Europe, and to some extent has made it so weak, but do we want, have we the right, to promote it when it will mean that many people lose their initial faith? If this book is meant to stem the process as a dam stands against the flood, the attempt will fail. No catechism, however well-intentioned, can hold up the movement of ideas. So should the book present the faith in the only terms in which it can be formulated after it has been exposed to scientific and historical criticism? Would that be a service to the people of the so-called 'Third World'? And could the message be clothed in the language of 'sound doctrine'?

The main problem of the Church today is a *panic* which is the last thing ordinary Catholics want. Synods, symposia, religious congresses, special holy years and much else are initiated without any questions about the relation of the means employed and the forces harnessed to the intended aims. When collected tranquillity for meditation on the faith is what we need, the Church is driven into a retreat forwards, as though its survival depended on the number of times it appeared in the headlines. The great danger of the new world catechism is that this book too will be launched on the world in a terrible panic. The wise special secretary to the synod made his specticism very clear.[8] Bishops and theologians the world over would be harassed for an over-hasty production of use to no-one. On the other hand, if the work is started with a serious programme—which is not quite inconceivable—for which this article has only been able to offer a few suggestions in passing, it is clear that it will not be completed either in this pontificate or in the next.

Translated by Francis McDonagh

Notes

1. Translator's note: The text given is translated from the German work cited in note 2. The version given in the *Tablet* (14 December 1985, p. 1326) englishes away some of the difficulties (see below, pp. 11ff.): 'There is a strong general wish for the writing of a catechism or compendium of the whole of Catholic doctrine, both on faith and morals, which could be a point of reference for the catechisms or compendiums composed in various areas. The manner of doctrinal presentation should be biblical and liturgical, offer sound teaching and be adapted to the life of Christians of today.'

2. *Zukunft aus der Kraft des Konzils. Die ausserordentliche Bischofssynode '85. Die Dokumente mit einem Kommentar* von W. Kasper (Freiburg-im-Breisgau, 1986), p. 83.

3. W. Kasper, the work cited in note 2, p. 84.

4. J. B. Metz's suggestions about how to make the Church genuinely polycentric are clearly relevant here.

5. See, for example, *Liturgie—ein vergessenes Thema der Theologie?* ed. K. Richter (Freiburg-im-Breisgau 1986).

6. W. Kasper, the work cited in note 2, p. 84.

7. One of the points made in a remarkably clear analysis of how the faith is transmitted today by the Archbishop of Paderborn, J. J. Degenhardt, 'Traditionskrise des Glaubens' in *Stimmen der Zeit* 111 (1986) 651–662, esp. 653.

8. W. Kasper, the work cited in note 2, pp. 84–85.

Alberto Moreira

Orthodoxy for the Protection of the Poor?

ON 21 MAY 1986, a 'Communication to the People of God' from the 11 bishops of the Brazilian state of Maranhão caused a disturbance throughout the country and far beyond. Ecclesiastical and political circles were astonished by the measure announced by the bishops. The Christian population and the press were officially informed that the Governor of Maranhão, Luiz Alvez Rocha, its Chief of Police,[1] Commandant João Silva Júnior, and the newspaper publisher of the Federation of Landowners, UDR[2] 'have cut themselves off from the community of the Church. There is no point if they show no signs of conversion in the true meaning of the Gospel'. The newspapers printed in bold headlines: Church excommunicates Governor.[3]

The astonishment is understandable when one considers that it was the first time in the history of the modern Brazilian Church, that *highly-placed political personalities had been chastised by the Church's strongest sanction.* Moreover, it came from the whole of the episcopacy. The situation is also astounding because those affected never ceased claiming they were still practising Catholics, even though Governor Rocha no longer wished 'to receive the host made of flour and the blood of the innocent, from the hands of murderers.' But he could not even begin to prove these accusations. The bishops, on the other hand, *had denounced institutionalised violence* in the country's interior some months before, in several pastoral letters. They had repeatedly gone to see the authorities to no avail, asking them to introduce measures against the encroachment by police and landowners on poverty-stricken farmers and those without land. Instead of legally prosecuting obvious crimes on the part of landowners, these authorities and the Governor himself accused the Church of 'subversively destroying order in the rural areas'.

The excommunication is astonishing and constitutes a precedent in a certain sense, because the bishops' official communication mentions none of the reasons which were traditionally the cause of excommunication: apostasy, schism, heresy, profanation of the eucharistic elements, violence against a bishop, blasphemy, etc. Certainly, those excommunicated were accused of having seriously defamed the Church (a sufficient cause for punishment according to Church law), but it is remarkable that the bishops give as the most important reasons for their decision facts which in European church publicity would possibly *count only as political or social offences:*

> Let these men compensate the population for the theft of land, for the impunity of those who have murdered labourers, for the razed villages, for inhumanity and the innumerable violations against the rights of men ... the cooperation between the State police of Maranhão and the politicians, whereby violent crime was organised ... In it (UDR) the landowners are organised, determined to protect their private possessions by whatever means and their domination over the land and over rural communities which are kept 'like cattle', in order to guarantee the (next political) vote. By making violent demands they take a stand against agricultural workers, rebel against agricultural reform, the Church and democracy.[4]

When, in the history of the Church, has actual behaviour, practice in ethical, social and political conflicts been regarded as the criterion for membership in the Church? Does the case presented and discussed here, of Brazil's agricultural conflict demonstrate the characterisation of Church law by Provost and Walf: that Church law (like every law) is inclined to be conservative and yet fulfills a prophetic function?[5]

The excommunication of politicians, high-ranking police officers and landowners by the bishops of Maranhão draws attention to the *land conflict in the north-east of Brazil.* Whereas in the history of the Church, excommunication has been used above all as the last weapon in the *defence of propositional truths,* here a pastoral practice of the Church is defended. This procedure has substantial implications for the theological understanding of the Church by itself, and its possible role in conflict situations. It also has significance for Church law. The procedure is also not simply 'political', despite evident political implications. In the eyes of the bishops, it belongs to their inmost theological and pastoral duties. This is something new and far-reaching in implication.

1. THE BACKGROUND OF THE EXCOMMUNICATION

The state of Maranhão, in the north-east, is about the size of France; 87.5 per cent of the *territory is concentrated in the hands of 19 owners of great ranches or latifundia*. The multitude of agricultural workers are poor posseiros, small scale farmers who have no title deed, although their rights are established by law. Expulsion and violence by armed members of the latifundian and political oligarchies form part of everyday life. Maranhão is a clear example of what is taking place in the rest of the country. In 1984, 12 agricultural workers were murdered there; in 1985, the figure was 22,222 in the whole of Brazil, many of whom were leaders of base communities and agricultural workers' unions. In May, 1986, the same month as the bishops' communication, a leading layman of Bacabal diocese, a Baptist minister and the priest Josimo Tavares were killed in Maranhão. The last mentioned was an active member of the Rural Pastoral Commission of the Church (CPT) who always acted without force and cautiously, but was denounced after his murder by the Chairman of the Federation of Landowners UDR (in his own words, 'a religious man') as a 'murderer, terrorist and guerilla leader'. Politicians and those in power feel inwardly strengthened at the thought that they are doing religion a good turn by operating in full force against 'communist priests'. *The official programme of agrarian 'reform' lacks political will, funds and sympathy* for the lot of the millions who are without land. In addition, the population of the north-east suffered one of the worst droughts of its history, claiming the lives of thousands of people, especially children. But the landowners hardly felt it, as they were supported by the state through various projects.

These are the people who have passed through the great ordeal (Rev. 7:14), a people tried by suffering and acquainted with illness (Isa. 53). But they are also a deeply religious people, who never lose hope and gather together into *base communities and various organisations, in order to fight against concrete oppression*. Land, for posseiros, is quite simply a chance for survival. Thus, the land question is not just a technical, political question; those affected experience it in the ethical and religious sphere. It is to this situation that the pastors address their words and they excommunicate the owner of the latifundium, the arrogance of the politicians, police violence and the lie printed in the paid press. In addition, on 11 June 1986, they called for three days' penitence and fasting for the whole population, against violence in Maranhão. What do the bishops wish to express with this excommunication?

2. IN THE SERVICE OF THE POOR, TO PROTECT ORTHODOXY

In a situation of institutionalised injustice, where Christians are oppressed and persecuted by 'Christians', where everything is 'turned on its head' and anything is allowed, the bishops (a) *first trace out the 'limits of Church membership'*. Not everything is acceptable. The Church has the ability and the pastoral responsibility to define itself *ex negativo* as well: this we are not; whoever acts in such and such a way cannot be a Christian, however much he claims the opposite. 'They try in vain to deceive the people by declaring themselves to be Christians standing wholeheartedly for peace and love.'

The pastors not only view themselves as under an obligation to watch over catholicity, they also see it as their pastoral duty repeatedly to define this catholicity in situations shot through with conflict: Where do we actually stand? In this way they rise above the unacceptability of a commodity culture impregnated with a capitalism that permeates all relationships and leads men to general indifference and numbness.

However, (b) *how do the bishops define Church membership?* They do not start from a purely legal, ecclesiastical point of view, rather, they start from a pastoral concern which begins among the poor. The bishops define the Church and membership in it from the perspective of a life of suffering with those deprived of their rights and those of least importance, that is, they start at the lowest level. And they do it in a strictly 'orthodox' way; that is to say, they take Christ's standards as the final criterion of catholicity and Christianity in general: 'Not everyone who calls me "Lord, Lord" will enter the kingdom of Heaven' (Matt. 7:21). And 'anything you did not do for one of these however humble, you did not do it for me' (Matt. 25:45).

(c) Thus, this punishment[6] of the political and social behaviour of the landowners and politicians betokens a *curse*, but it asks them for 'public signs of conversion in the true meaning of the Gospel'. Excommunication denies blessing to the powerful—that blessing which only falls on those who show solidarity with the victims and contribute to the strengthening of faith among the poor, who have converted to become one of the privileged in the true meaning of the Gospel. The impulse of this excommunication arises neither from the outdated polemic between Church and enlightened State, in which as a 'societas perfecta' it makes use of a *ius coactivum* to secure its own position.[7] The bishops start from the theological recognition that the *faith of the poor is also a criterion for the Church's truth*. Whoever attacks this truth will at the same time strike one of the fundaments of the Church and of Christianity. '...it would be better for him to have a millstone hung round his neck and be drowned in the depths of the sea' (Matt. 18:6).

3. IMPLICATIONS FOR SOCIETY, CHURCH AND ECCLESIASTICAL LAW

The main point of this excommunication appears in the *social sphere*. Governor, Chief of Police and newspaper publisher are eminent social functions. They ought to provide a model of the 'right' way to treat others. First, the bishops reject the dualism—characteristic for bourgeois society—of social behaviour and personal responsibility. They 'excommunicate' the existing dichotomy in the life of society and the Church, between personal piety and socially responsible behaviour. Second, not only did Governor Rocha, Commandant Silva Júnior and the newspaper publisher of the UDR violate a paragraph of the Church's law (i.e. severe calumny against the Church), they set themselves actively and passively against an apparently 'purely human' law (of land reform) which literally constituted a question of life and death for millions of landless and posseiros. *A social question (the rights of the poor to a worthwhile life) penetrates to the innermost identity of the Church*, to the extent that an attitude which rejects the Church will finally constitute a sufficient and adequate criterion for exclusion from it:

(i) Christian faith contains a dimension of social responsibility which is also decisive for Church membership.

(ii) Socially responsible behaviour (in politics, trade, insurance, the formation of public opinion) belongs to the inner, identifying structure of Christian community.

(iii) The orthodoxy of Christian community is preserved when Church membership is defined and avowed according to Jesus' standards, from the wrong side of the fabric of history, from the point of men of the impoverished and excluded. The Church is then experienced as a community, as the people of God in communion with the victims.

(iv) Specific people have placed themselves outside the community; what they represent and defend is also a contradiction of community: the latifundium, that fence which divides human beings into hungry beggars and fat property owners—an ultimately unjust social system.

(v) Viewed from within, the bishops reinforce the faith of the poor and give support for their liberating activities. Seen from outside, the Church functions as an ideological critic of a power which only pursues its own interests. It disavows the ideological reinterpretation of religious symbols in 'political speech', by pointing to the fruits of the behaviour of politicians and media men in society. They speak of peace, development and security, but it is conflict which springs up, the suffering of the poor, and general, all-round lack of security.

The case of the excommunication of politicians, landowners and rulers in Brazil shows that Church identity is endangered *not only by false, erroneous consciousness, but also by the practice of oppression.* The truth of Christian faith is never to be found simply in the faith held (Metz), never abstractly as a phenomenon for consciousness divorced from concrete practice; the whole truth of faith encompasses practical activity as well, material reality; orthodoxy always implies orthopraxis at the same time. In the evidence of the Church in Maranhão a richer, more complete meaning of orthodoxy begins to become visible.

Translated by Jane Curran

Notes

1. Literally, Secretary for Public Security.
2. União Democrática Ruralista, Democratic Land Union, founded 1984, with links to organised crime and gun running.
3. The sentence is not precisely defined as excommunication or as interdict. However, the people and the press immediately took it to mean excommunication. The legal basis used appears to have been Canons 1369, 1370 and 1374 of the CIC.
4. German translation: 'Brasilien Ausschnittdienst' (Mettingen 1986) 6, p. 41.
5. See *Concilium* 185 (3/1986) 'Canon Law—Church Reality' eds. J. Provost and K. Walf. Editorial, at pp. ix–x.
6. On this point, see L. Gerosa 'Penal Law and Ecclesiastica! Reality in *Concilium* 185 (3/1986) 54–63.
7. E. Corecco 'Ecclesiological Bases of the Code' in *Concilium* 185 (3/1986) 3–13.
8. See S. Bwana 'The Impact of the New Code in Africa' in *Concilium* 185 (3/1986) 103–109.

Dorothee Sölle

'The Moment of Truth'. The Kairos Document from Africa

THE KAIROS DOCUMENT of South African and for the most part Black Christians is a *document of Church history* of the last quarter of the century the status of which can scarcely be over-estimated.[1] It satisfies three conditions of present-day theological effort which are reflected precisely in *Concilium* topics over the last few years.

First, it is a *model for the magisterium of the faithful*, who offer a theological commentary on political conflict in their area and, partly with and partly against the official *magisterium* of their churches, represent thus the majority of an oppressed people. The document was received with enthusiasm in the Black townships, but even the South African Catholic bishops' conference welcomed it as a 'vision of hope' and recommended their parishes to read it. Twenty-four of the initial signatories are Roman Catholics; this is impressive when one remembers that Catholics in South Africa are in the minority.

Its very clear, biblically unflinching language gives the document a natural authority wholly appropriate to the *magisterium* of the faithful. It speaks that language of the 'organic intellectual' which Gramsci dreamed of, and therefore meets with fierce criticism from many White Protestant church leaders, who have called it an 'incitement to anarchy, which is always worse than the worst tyranny'.[2]

Second, Kairos is a first-class *example of the essential bond between orthopraxis and orthodoxy*. The group met at the centre of that town of two million inhabitants that does not appear on South African maps—in Soweto. It came together at the beginning of the civil unrest which it saw as 'the moment of truth and crisis', not only for apartheid 'but for the Church'. It

116

takes seriously the summons to action (chapter 5), which it studies and exemplifies in the historically apt location.

'In June 1985, when the crisis came to a head throughout the country, and a constantly growing number of people were killed, silenced and imprisoned; when one Black township after the other rebelled against the apartheid régime; when people—facing death from day to day—turned against oppression and refused to co-operate with the oppressors; and when the army of apartheid forced its way into the townships in order to maintain its rule with guns: theologians concerned by the situation met in their need to grasp the state of things appropriately and to consider what was the right and due reaction of the Church and of all Christians in South Africa' (Foreword).

Third, the Kairos document *examines precisely the set of problems arising from the conflict between orthodoxy and heterodoxy*, though that terminology is not used. I think that the authors' most important intellectual effort is to understand and to try to come to terms with the core of the socio-political conflict in its theological dimension. What is actually in question is a 'theological civil war in South Africa', as one Dutch daily said. *Christians are in different camps.* For instance, Church leaders such as Andries Treurnicht and Caral Boshoff are on the White side; and Desmond Tutu and Alan Boesak are on the Black side. In the light of the heresy practised in South Africa today, the question of a right or a wrong situation, or for varying viewpoints and opinions, is no longer a matter of expected variance within a Church. Here it is no longer a question of opinions about the Virgin Birth or the literal nature of the creation narrative.

In this conflict orthodoxy and heresy become a matter of life and death, for the continued existence of thousands of people is decided on their basis. Every Christian policeman who fires into an 'assembly' of school children participates in the heresy of apartheid, as much as every West German banker who provides the financial means to maintain the bankrupt system.

You do not have to be especially orthodox in order to discover—together with the ecumenical movement—that *apartheid is 'heresy'*. But it is interesting that this theological insight could emerge in the churches of the Reformation, although the bourgeois-liberal conceptual model believed for a long time that it was above the orthodoxy-heterodoxy divide. The seventeenth–eighteenth century disputes between orthodoxy and heterodoxy were lost struggles conducted, on the one hand, by ecclesiastical orthodoxy against scientific biblical criticism—and critical thought in general—and on the other hand, delimitations of the living devotion of Pietism. This liberal—in the best sense of the word—possibility of solving the problem of orthodoxy versus heterodoxy has now reached its historical culmination. There can be no tolerance between the practitioners of apartheid and their victims and opponents. Apartheid—and the heresies of racism and anti-Communism which are behind it—cannot be reformed, diminished or humanised. It has to be got rid of, because it represents the project of death in our world.

When I speak of the *'historical culmination' of a specific form of liberalism and its toleration*, I am thinking of first-world Christians, who nowadays make much use of the rhetoric of tolerance and do so precisely in their churches, in order to tone down the attack on the heresies from which they profit so much. Those subjected to colonialism in the third world have known for some time that not all people behave to one another as children of God and as brothers and sisters! For Black slaves in the USA certain parts of the Bible—such as Gal. 3:28—were meaningless for a long time. In terms of Church history, in Europe the beginning of Fascism marked the end of the liberal era, and it is not accidental that very orthodox formulations of Christian thought, such as that of the 'status confessionis', arose and bore fruit in Christian resistance movements against Fascism. *The bourgeoisie had trivialised the confrontation between orthodoxy and heterodoxy.* It was only with the shock provoked by the ideological power of Fascist heresy, which denied the human rights of certain social groups (Jews, gypsies, homosexuals), that consideration of 'right doctrine', a proper attitude to life and due action resurfaced. This end of a liberal appeasement, which nullified evil, and looked on the project of death (which signifies the existing world economic order as far as the poor are concerned) as reformable, is most clearly apparent today in the liberation struggles of the third world. There, as nowhere else nowadays, 'true doctrine' concerning the creation, liberation, and right relations is current. In spite of all false spiritualisation, here the Bible is needed with its outspokenness on the class question, and its realism about powers and dominions, demons and compulsions; here there is a predominant *hunger for true doctrine*: that is, the sole prerequisite which can legitimise an orthodoxy is present here.

The Kairos document belongs to this context. It is in the tradition of the Confessing Church in the Nazi period, which in its Barmen Declaration of 1934 made a similar attempt—which must nevertheless be seen as inadequate because it was inappropriate to the situation of the Jews under persecution by the Nazis. But it is in Bonhoeffer, whom the community of the Confessing Church did not follow as far as it ought to have done, that the notion of 'status confessionis' recurred, which the Church found itself facing as a result of State action that forced a group of people into a lawless condition.[3] For Christians, *'status confessionis' means the necessity of turning against and resisting the dominant injustice proclaimed or tolerated by the State*, and thus publicly 'confessing' or acknowledging one's adherence to Christ. Wherever the state forces Christians to burn incense to Caesar, public acknowledgment becomes a necessary form of expression of Christian faith, which extends beyond prayer, bible reading or divine service. Burning incense to Caesar could mean, in the Nazi period, for instance, propagating Nazi racism, as when a shopkeeper had to hang a card saying 'No Jews!' in his window. In Johannesburg the pinch of incense for Caesar means obeying the rules of apartheid and the laws of injustice; in Hamburg or London it means preparing for war and stockpiling the weapons of mass destruction through co-operation and payment of taxes.

Does a 'status confessionis' of this kind, which in recent discussions is also referred to sometimes as 'processus confessionis'[4], exist in the South African situation? In 1977, at its plenary assembly in Dar es Salam, the Lutheran World Federation declared a 'status confessionis' in regard to the South African policy of separation of the races and its ecclesiastical effects; in 1982 the Reformed World Federation followed the same course. This confession is in its way an expression of orthodoxy-orthopraxis. To be sure, some member churches and parishes still sense a degree of enactment and prescription from above. Nothing like that is to be found in the Kairos document. The fact that 'the Church is divided' and that 'its day of judgment has dawned' is the fundamental thesis of the first chapter ('The Moment of Truth'). The document is an example of a orthodoxy-orthopraxis 'from below', which is also a challenge to the official churches.

The kairos theologians distinguish three different theologies, which they categorise as '*State theology*', '*church theology*' and '*prophetic theology*'. This division is, I think, more useful than that emanating from academic circles which represents the distinction as one between 'orthodoxy', 'liberalism' and 'liberation theology'.[5] The kairos theologians name the *bearers or agents of the theologies* in their partition. They locate the theologies in their material context.

With *State theology* they indicate a looming phenomenon which has to do with far more than the South African racists, and which by no means disappeared long ago in other Western countries. On the contrary, a State ideology, a kind of 'civil religion' or national consensus, together with declarations of faith in the constitution of the State or the irrefragable necessity of militarism and other aspects, is becoming ever more evident. On the basis of my own experiences in West Germany, I would say that we also have a form of 'State theology', even though it is less primitive and violent than in South Africa, yet in cases of conflict presents as 'defence' and uses as its means demarcations and segregations, tear gas and rubber bullets. State theology misuses theological concepts and biblical texts for its own political ends. The kairos theologians cite four key examples to show this in practice in South Africa.

> 'The first is the use of Romans 13:1–7, whereby the State is to be accorded an absolute divine authority. The second is the use of the term "law and order" in order to decide and control what the people are to look on as just or unjust. The third example is the use of the word "Communist" to brand anyone who speaks out against the "State theology". Finally there is the way in which the name of God is used' (chapter 2).

Therefore exegetical, religion-critical, ideology-critical and in the narrower sense theo-logical methods are used to fulfil what according to the Reformers is the most important task of theology: that is, *to distinguish between God and idols*. The State idol also claims a biblical foundation, and calls on Romans 13 in variation after variation, in order to sell Christians the idea of blind obedience and absolute subjection to the State as the will of God! *Law and order* then have the function of confirming 'ordained' exploitation, or 'legally regulated oppression', as binding in conscience. On the contrary, the Kairos theologians say: 'Something does not become moral and just merely because the State has made it a law; and the organisation of a society does not represent a just and due order merely because it was introduced by the State' (2.2). This description of 'civil religion', as State theology is usually called in the bourgeois democracies, exactly fits the consciousness of the majority of Christians, even in countries which do not use the law to secure their racism. This applies even more to the third pillar of state theology. 'Like any other theology, "state theology" must also have its own concrete symbol for evil. It has to have its own version of hell. And so it has found—or, rather, adopted—the myth of Communism. Everything that is evil is Communist, and all Communist or socialist ideas are atheistic and godless' (2.3). In this way, in South Africa today, millions of above all Black Christians are classed as 'atheists'.

Anti-Communism is the basic principle of State theology; it is no less heretical than the ideology of apartheid itself. By means of its Manichaean notion of the universe with its rending of creation, it takes the place of God, 'knows the roots of all evil' and is the god of advanced technology. As the Kairos theologians say in a passage which has already become famous,

> 'It is the god of "casspirs" and "hippos" (armoured military vehicles used in the townships), the god of tear gas, rubber bullets, rhino whips, prison cells and death sentences. Here is a god that hath exalted the proud and hath put down the humble and meek—the exact opposite of the God of the Bible' (2.4).

Yet again: the images which are used here to represent the god of State theology arise from the actual South African situation, and in other parts of the world there are other avatars of this god, which embody oppressive power pure and simple. But there are other instances—for example,the universally practised militarisation of society—where the reality of the all-ordaining idol is transfigured in just as religious a manner, and is used to brainwash people with the help of an absolutely unthinking anti-Communism.

The third chapter of the document criticises 'church theology' and refers essentially to the English-speaking churches of South Africa. Their theology may be described as liberal and idealist; their God is non-partisan and palliates everything. The most important watchwords of this theology are reconciliation, justice which must come about on the basis of 'personal conversion' or a 'moral summons', and non-violence, the most contested term. 'How is it possible', the Kairos theologians ask, 'to censure all use of force and yet to appoint military chaplains to serve in an extremely violent and oppressive army? How can one condemn the use of force and yet permit young White men to accept their call-up to the armed forces? Is it because the use of police and army is seen as defensive?' (3.3).

The god behind this Church theology is the 'deus ex machina' whom Bonhoeffer criticised: the omnipotent Father and Lord, criticised by feminist theology, who does not act in and with us, but intervenes from above and is essentially above all parties. In addition, the Kairos theologians' critique of South African church theology fits precisely the consensus theology of the first world. It sees sin as irreconcilability, whereas for State theology sin is rebellion against the power of the State.

In the sense of the last-mentioned 'prophetic theology' to which we only approximate, sin is something quite different: it is oppression itself, that fundamental structural category of a biblical theology in which we participate as oppressors or as those who hope to belong to their ranks, or as the oppressed. Here too the historical-materialist approach of the Kairos document is apparent.

'The Bible describes oppression as human experience in which people are trampled on, devalued, humiliated, exploited, impoverished, deceived, led astray and enslaved. The oppressors are represented as cruel, indifferent, arrogant, greedy, violent, tyrannical and satanic. Such descriptions could emanate only from people who have experienced a long and painful oppression. In fact almost 90 per cent of the history of the Jewish people and later of Christians related in the Bible is the history of national or international oppression' (4.2).

Oppression as experience is a fundamental criterion for distinguishing prophetic from Church theology. In the Bible the notion of oppression has some twenty different names. Only if we emerge from our bourgeois non-partiality and take that seriously do we also see the necessity of 'distinguishing the signs of the time' (Matt. 16:3): that is, conceive a thorough analysis of the socio-political situation as a part of God's revelation to us. A State which turns itself into the enemy of the people, the oppressor of justice, cannot be 'reconciled', as many Church theologians still maintain is possible. The god of such a State is 'the devil, disguised as almighty God—in fact, the anti-Christ' (2.4).

I want to return for a moment to the question of *why apartheid is heresy, or how the theological distinction between orthodoxy and heterodoxy helps us to understand reality*. The conception of apartheid itself is theologically derived (it is all too justifiable to subject it to theological criticism). But there has been some change here. In earlier years in South Africa there was discussion whether apartheid could be justified biblically. The story of the Tower of Babel, so it was claimed, indicated the will of God that the various nations (and skin pigmentations) should develop separately. The curse on Ham and his descendants justified the greater value and higher position of the 'baas-skap', the superiority of the White group of peoples. This theology would seem to have become irrelevant for those now in power. Today the reference is usually only to the irrefragable sovereignty of the State and the subjection of its underlings.

In 1982, in a theological declaration, the *Anglican Church in South Africa* pronounced apartheid to be false doctrine: 'Apartheid elevates a biological characteristic to the status of a universally comprehensive principle and thus denies that the infinite dignity of human beings consists in the fact that they are created in the image of God (Gen. 1:27). By asserting the irreconcilability of different races, apartheid denies a central Christian teaching: namely, that God has reconciled the world to himself through Christ. Apartheid has caused human suffering to an irresponsible degree. Therefore we decided that apartheid is wholly unChristian, evil and a heresy'.[6]

But this same special feature of South Africa is to be found in the entire culture of the first world. Just as there is apartheid tourism, in which the unsullied beaches of South Africa are publicised, so there is also an apartheid theology which seeks to make the poor invisible and to replace the category of sin, that is oppression, with bourgeois individualism, as a limit-condition of first-world theology. The Kairos theologians have a relation to truth which differs from that usually predominant in the first-world churches. *They need truth, true doctrine, orthodoxy—they hunger for it.* Without hunger the truth is reduced to the category of an orthodoxy established solely on domination. With this hunger, guided by this hunger, the Church becomes the social location where human truth and beauty can be expressed. Finally, God needs these women and men together with their hunger.

Translated by J. G. Cumming

Notes

1. *Das KAIROS Document. Ein theologischer Kommentar zur politischen Krise in Südafrika* (Hamburg 1986).
2. See W. Weisse 'Gerechtigkeit von unten. KAIROS diskussion in Südafrika' *Ev. Komm.* 5/86 (Stuttgart).
3. D. Bonhoeffer *Gesammelte Schriften*, III (Münich) p. 246.
4. W. Huber *Folgen christlicher Freiheit. Ethik und Theorie der Kirche im Horizont der Barmer Theologischen Erklärung* (Vluyn 1983) pp. 249ff.
5. D. Sölle 'Die drei Theologien'. in: L. & W. Schottroff *Wer is unser Gott? Beiträge zu einer Befreiungstheologie im Kontext der 'Ersten' Welt* (Münich 1986).
6. Quoted in de Gruchy, John *'Wenn wir wie Brüder beieinander wohnten ...'* ed. Villa-Vicencio, Charles (Neukirchen 1984).

François Biot

The Idea of Orthodoxy in Cardinal Ratzinger's Book: Conversation on the Faith

SUMMARY

THE CONVERSATION on the Faith is a fight against the many heresies rampant today. The most serious and fundamental of these heresies is about the nature of the Church, reducing it to nothing but the collective of believers. In order to combat this heresy and those that flow from it, Cardinal Ratzinger proposes as his sovereign remedy the Virgin Mary. However, attributing such a role to Mary means removing her from her human historical condition and in a way hypostasising her. The orthodoxy maintained is safeguarded by authority for the benefit of the poor and weak, but without any active participation on their part. Orthodoxy, like Truth, is detached from cultural involvement. It has no real relation to history, even that of believers. It is given. We do not make it.

From the very first pages of his Conversation on the Faith Cardinal Ratzinger presents himself as the depositary of catholic orthodoxy by virtue of his very position. Throughout these 250 pages the theme of orthodoxy is constant. To assess the scope of this work, to which the Cardinal Prefect of the Congregation for the Doctrine of the Faith seems to have attached very great importance, we need to try to define his concept of orthodoxy and the role this fundamental concept plays for him.

We should make two preliminary remarks.

First, the Conversation on the Faith is the result of an interview lasting many hours and published in a form where it is not usually possible to distinguish Vittorio Messori's thoughts from Joseph Ratzingers's. Certainly there are sometimes quotations from the cardinal or his previous published texts and these are introduced by inverted commas, or *ipsissima verba* also in inverted commas. Sometimes the cardinal's thoughts are reported in indirect speech. Sometimes the interview also gives Messori's own views or reactions. However, for the most part, the book is written in a single voice, that of the Ratzinger-Messori duo. With some reservations and regrets we decided to accept the text as it is. This is the text we have used to define the cardinal's notion of orthodoxy and its function. Thus our attempted interpretation is not directly of the cardinal's thought but of the content of this work, which he has signed and the distribution of which he explicitly authorised as faithful and in line with his own positions and views.

A second difficulty of interpretation arises from the many implicit or half explicit references justifying or explaining Ratzinger's positions. He often refers to *certain* theologians, *certain* trends, *certain exegetes*, *certain* priests etc without ever giving any precise data about author, work, circumstances and passages condemned. In order to understand him fully, it is indispensable to know exactly what and who he is talking about. Perhaps it might be said that in this way the cardinal did not want to stoop to personal polemic (except with his former colleague from the Tübingen Theology Faculty, who is easily identifiable because Ratzinger quotes from his work *Goodbye to the Devil*). However, the trouble with this lack of precision is that it throws suspicion on every theologian, every exegete, every catechist etc.

In order to grasp Ratzinger's concept of orthodoxy, we shall begin by studying very briefly what he opposes it to: the manifold heresies or errors denounced all the way through his work *Conversation on the Faith*. Then we shall see how orthodoxy triumphs over these heresies and errors. Then we shall try to discover what function Ratzinger assigns to orthodoxy in order to arrive at his notion of Truth, which is at the heart of his concept of orthodoxy.

1. A WORLD OF HERESIES

Today there are many errors and heresies which are against orthodoxy. The *Conversation on the Faith* exposes them at length. The most fundamental heresy, which is at the root of all the evil and which has jeopardised the hoped-for fruits of Vatican II, is a *heresy about the Church*. This heresy considers the Church as a human construction, an instrument created by us: the *collective* of believers (p. 50).

Ratzinger adds that in this view the logical sequence leads from a purely human structure to a purely human project: '*The Gospel becomes the Jesus-project, the project of social liberation or other purely immanent historical projects, which may still seem religious but are in fact atheist in their substance*' (p. 51).

For Ratzinger this heresy slinks in perniciously under the term *Church as the people of God*, which was of course used by Vatican II. But at Vatican II the expression was explicitly used in relation with other expressions such as the Church as the body of Christ. The unilateral insistence on the Church as the people of God makes Ratzinger fear a return to the Old Testament or even a tendency towards '*partisan collectivist political ideas ...*' (p. 52).

This tendency is also manifested in the attribution to the Church itself of its members' sins, whereas, according to Ratzinger, the Church so transcends those who are its members that it remains always holy and a communion of '*holy things*'.

This heresy is expressed in particular in *liberation theology*, as Ratzinger understands it. This theology adopts the immanentist conception, which consists in ascribing to human efforts to free ourselves a real capacity to achieve positive and effective results: '*It is precisely this history-bound visions with no outlet to the transcendent which has led humanity to its present predicament*' (p. 212). But it also expresses itself in many heresies which touch upon all aspects of Christian doctrine.

2. TRIUMPH OVER HERESIES

In order to triumph over present heresies there is no better remedy in Cardinal Ratzinger's opinion than the one that conquered the heresies of the past: the Virgin Mary proclaimed since the early centuries as *victorious over all heresies*.

Indeed the Virgin Mary plays a decisive part in the balance and achievement of the Catholic faith. This argument is developed at length.

The difficulty is in knowing what the cardinal means. Does he mean discerning in the whole content of Catholic faith a specific role, for example, a role of synthesis, for dogmatic statement about Mary? This is the primary sense which emerges. For example the *Conversation on the Faith* proclaims that '*recognising the place given by dogma and tradition to Mary means being solidly rooted in authentic Christology*' (p. 124). In this case a truly Catholic Christology—dogmatically and traditionally—is guaranteed and authenticated in traditional dogmatic statement about Mary. This interpretation appears, on the one hand, in the statement that the Marian dogmas perfectly integrate scripture and tradition, and, on the other, in the praise of Marian *devotion*, which pre-eminently maintains the balance of faith between reason and feeling. However even here another consideration arises, not of faith and its content but of the role of Mary herself in the *history of salvation*.

This second point leads to the following reflection. Mary's personal history appears as exemplary and typical: a young Jewish girl became the Messiah's mother and so she belongs to both the Old and the New Testaments.[1] She unites one to the other in her own person. Moreover because she is both virgin and mother, she is the pre-eminent model of womanhood in God's plan but also typical as signifying God's action, *'which can intervene freely even in matter'* (p. 125).

Hence we must distinguish two different levels of understanding. The first concerns the content of faith, happily balanced and achieved through articles of faith (or devotion) bearing on Mary. The second, deeper level shows how Mary's person justified the role of balance and achievement performed by Marian dogmas: her own place in the *history of salvation*.

Christology, the relation between scripture and tradition, reason and feeling, are balanced and achieved by the dogmatic statements on Mary. Old and New Testaments, God's creative and providential action, including his action on matter, and the Catholic view of woman, are signified and manifested in the model that Mary embodied in the *history of salvation*.

On the first level we note that Ratzinger is arguing in a circle. Faith finds its balance and achievement in the dogma and tradition about Mary. In other words, orthodoxy about Mary confirms and achieves the orthodoxy of Christology, the relation between scripture and tradition, the balance between reason and feeling (domain of devotion). Orthodoxy calls to orthodoxy, just as it supports and achieves it. It would be difficult to find a better description of the *systematic character of Catholic doctrine*, in which truths support each other, thus enabling the whole structure to stand.

We leave aside the many questions that might be raised about the fact that the materials used for the actual building may include elements extraneous to the faith, such as cultural elements or even historical events. These questions are completely beyond Ratzinger's scope.

Confining ourselves to him and his schema, we note that this systematic circle, in which orthodoxy confirms and achieves orthodoxy, rests on a different reality, that is the person of Mary and her destiny in God's plan. It is clear that at this basic level Ratzinger does not in fact appeal to actual happenings: the facts about Mary and what she did, but to her objective situation, which is of another order.

Structurally she is situated at the juncture of the Old and New Testaments. Structurally she is virgin and mother. It is only in passing that the cardinal refers to any particular behaviour or attitude of hers and then only to propose her as a model for Christians.

Hence we see how the system of dogmatic and devotional orthodoxy functions. In order for her to be the basis of the circle of orthodoxy, Mary's story must be *de-historicised*. Indeed her story is not a succession of events in which human decision has a part to play; it is the object of God's plan and remains within these structures.

This is the way Ratzinger connects the role played by Marian dogmas in the faith and the role of Mary as a person with a particular destiny. For fear that *praxis* could in some way or another become the basis of orthodoxy, Ratzinger is led to *de-historicise Mary's actual story*. So the question arises whether he is talking about Mary 'in the flesh', as she appears in the Gospel texts or rather—as we would suggest—about what might be called a '*hypostasis*' not belonging to the historical domain but to the divine world as one of its manifestations, and passing through history without being in any way affected by a wholly provisional sojourn in the human world.[2]

3. FUNCTION OF ORTHODOXY

After these considerations on the hypostasised and symbolic figure of orthodoxy represented by Mary, let us go on to the *role which Ratzinger assigns to orthodoxy*. We can distinguish two aspects. The first is strategic, the second more fundamental.

First of all he is concerned to defend the poor against the dangers of illusory ideas, which might lead them to believe that their liberation could be achieved through human freedom forces. In a reaction against the stress laid by current theological tendencies such as liberation theology or even by pastoral trends on the *preferential option for the poor*, Ratzinger glories in his own more authentic and loyal service to the poor. At least he stops them having illusions followed by a painful awakening. In other words, it is a question of respecting the rights of the believing community of the simple faithful, who take priority over the rights of theologians.

However, this service is perceived and presented as a pastoral duty and the only thing the faithful have to do about it is submit. But preventing the poor from being bamboozled by illusions means supposing they are easily duped by novelties, because they lack knowledge, perspicacity and wisdom. Thus we see Ratzinger's hierarchical view of the service of Truth. The teaching Church transmits its knowledge to the taught church. The idea that the poor themselves can have an experience of faith in their own community and therefore have something to *teach* the guardians of orthodoxy is completely foreign to such a hierarchical view.

More fundamentally, orthodoxy is the guardian of what Ratzinger calls the *depositum fidei*, which he thinks the Congregation for the Doctrine of the Faith is in charge of. Christianity, the cardinal explains, is not *'from us'*. It is *'a revelation, that is to say a message which has been entrusted to us as a deposit and which we do not have the right to reconstruct according to our whims'* (p. 112).

That is why the task of the theologian is not to create but to explain the deposit of faith. And that is also why the catechist's mission is not to present this or that aspect of the truth suited to our time or cultural situation, but to transmit the 'core': what must be believed, what must be hoped and what must be done. The hierarchy and in particular the Congregation for the Doctrine of Faith have a duty to oversee the correct accomplishment of these tasks.

Nevertheless the deposit of faith is to be understood as the whole edifice of Catholic dogma, including of course recently defined dogmas such as papal infallibility or the assumption of the virgin Mary. Thus we should not interpret the deposit of faith as the 'hard core' already present in the New Testament churches and which is still the foundation of the whole building today.

The deposit of faith insists on the *objective data which constitute the Church's body of doctrine*, in opposition to so-called modernist perspectives, which stress the paramount importance of subjective ways of making the faith our own, and which recognise a not merely external and accidental but consubstantial link between the confession of faith and the believer's own cultural and subjective conditions. In this respect Ratzinger's affirmation is highly significant: it makes the Church and not the persons who constitute the Church as a social group, the *subject* of faith. The result of this is that adhering to the Church as a system of belief is a necessary precondition to participation in the faith, since this is an act of the Church.[3]

Thus orthodoxy's essential function is to ensure that believers, including theologians, believe what the Church believes and not seek to make God's living word their own in a personal—and thus partial—way. In this respect orthodoxy's aim is to *objectify* the faith. Not to *de-privatise* but to *depersonalise* it. In the last resort what each of us has as our own is our wretchedness and sin. (See esp. p. 56.)

4. TRUTH IS NOT OF HUMAN ORIGIN

There remains one last point to be made about how Ratzinger conceives truth. '*Truth*,' he writes, '*is a fundamental element in human life*' (p. 21). And he goes on to say, '*We cannot find Truth or create it*' (p. 69).

Such formulae are not merely naive. They are his actual stand points on difficult questions. Let us look at just two of these questions because of their importance for the very idea of orthodoxy.

Firstly there is the question of the relation between *orthopraxy* and *orthodoxy*. The cardinal prefect vigorously denounces what he sees as heretical: '*What matters today is only orthopraxy, that is to say behaving rightly and loving our neighbour. Orthodoxy in the sense of believing rightly in the true Scriptural sense in accordance with the Church's living Tradition is therefore viewed as secondary, even alienating. A facile slogan because it is so superficial …*' (p. 22). For him it is obvious that right action presupposes right thinking. And this right thinking is Truth with a capital T, '*which can be known, expressed and, up to a point, defined in a precise manner*' (p. 23).

Truth is divine. It is the object of God's revelation, which he has entrusted to the Church. The cardinal in no way accepts that this revelation is made through history, that is to say through a body of actions, especially those of Jesus, which carry special significance. According to him it is as if Truth was first spoken before it was lived, not vice versa, in spite of all biblical experience to the contrary.

Secondly, there is the question of what access believers of today have to the truth or rather God's word. Thus on the matter of belief in the personal existence of Satan, Ratzinger remarks that, '*We are assured that these forms of thought are no longer compatible with our way of seeing the world today … what is considered to be incomprehensible to the average person today is thrown out*' (p. 174).

Of course modern civilisation is not the final criterion. But we see from this how Ratzinger is ignorant of the subjective conditions for knowing the truth. As if it were sufficient for the Truth to be '*in itself*' in order for it to be true '*for us*'.

Thus we come back to the same viewpoints, which tend to confirm the hypothesis we advanced on the subject of Mary, and on the Church. Truth is conceived as divine, episodically coming down into our human world without in any way becoming involved with us.

Thus orthodoxy itself is also to be understood as a sort of non-historical '*hypostasis*', entrusted to the Church as the subject of genuine faith.

And entrusted in particular to the Congregation for the Doctrine of Faith. It has no real relation with history, even believers' history, even that of its witnesses, or even indeed the principal witness, the man Jesus. Progressively making the word of God our own has no theological significance because Truth is not to be made but only to be received and kept as a deposit.

Translated by Dinah Livingstone

Notes

1. Mary's belonging to both Testaments seems to be considered by Ratzinger as a situation unique to her. However it is first and foremost Jesus' own situation and also that of the first Christian communities, which grew up through the apostles' preaching and which were also at the juncture between the Old and New Testaments.

2. We consider this hypothesis a key to the interpretation of the *Conversation on the Faith*. In Cardinal Ratzinger's view, the Church in particular is a divine reality to the point where real history has no explicit part to play at all in its structure. The Church goes through history without any involvement in the human world.

3. Christians belong to the Church, which is the *subject* of faith. Ratzinger avoids the *historical* perspective of the Church as the community of those who believe in God's word.

Contributors

GIUSEPPE ALBERIGO was born in Varese in 1926 and lectures in History at the Faculty of Political Studies of Bologna University. He is also Secretary of the Institute for Religious Studies in Bologna, Editor of the quarterly Review *Cristianesimo nella storia* and a member of the International editorial committee of *Concilium*. His published books include works on the Council of Trent, the development of the concept of power in the church, collegiality and Pope John XXIII, the genesis of *Lumen gentium*, Conciliarism and the reception of Vatican II.

FRANÇOIS BIOT, OP, was born in Lyons in 1923 in a family of twelve children. His father was a doctor and involved at the time in social catholicism. He joined the Dominicans in 1942 and was ordained priest in 1949. He studied Reformation History at the Institut für Europäische Geschichte at Mayence. Then he took part in ecumenical research. In 1962 he became advisory theologian to the journal *Témoignage Chrétien* and in this capacity went to Rome to follow the four sessions of the Second Vatican Council. He also worked as an adviser to several bishops. At the same time he continued teaching theology in the Dominican Convent of Studies for the province of Lyons. At present he is director of the periodical *Exchanges* and president of Espace Barthélémy de las Casas for solidarity and cultural exchange with the peoples of Latin America. His publications include *Communautés protestantes* (1959); *De la polémique au dialogue* (1963); *En route vers l'unité* (1965); *Théologie du politique* (1972); *L'Evangile n'est pas neutre* (1974); *Le Corbusier et l'architecture sacrée* (1985); *Lève-toi et marche. Réponse au Ratzinger* (1985).

IRING FETSCHER was born in 1922 in Marbach/Neckar. He studied at the universities of Tübingen and Paris (1945–51) and obtained his first doctorate in 1950 with a thesis on Hegel's anthropology. In 1959 he obtained his professorial doctorate with a thesis on Rousseau's political philosophy. Since 1963 he has been professor of political science and social philosophy at the university of Frankfurt am Main. He is also visiting professor at the universities of Göttingen, Nijmegen, Tel Aviv and the Graduate Faculty of the New School for Social Research in New York. His main books include *Von Marx zur Sowjetideologie* (23rd enlarged ed. 1981), *Karl Marx et le Marxisme* (1967) and *Überlebensbedingungen der Menschheit* (1980).

ANTON HOUTEPEN was born in 1940 and studied theology in Hoeven, Nijmegen and Heidelberg. He is now Professor of Fundamental Theology at the Erasmus Institute in Rotterdam and Director of the Ecumenical Department of the Interuniversity Instituut voor Missiologie en Oecumenica at Utrecht. His publications include: *Onfeilbaarheid en Hermeneutiek* (1973); *Theology of the 'Saeculum'* (1976); 'Lehrautorität in der oekumenischen Diskussion' in *Verbindliches Lehren der Kirche heute. Beiheft zum Oekumenischen Rundschau* 33 (1978) 120–208; *People of God. A Plea for the Church* (1984); *De Petrusdienst van de bisschop van Rome* (1985); *In God is geen geweld* (1985).

JAMES F. McCUE is Professor of Religion at the University of Iowa (Iowa City, Iowa) and Director of the Program in Global Studies at that university. His publications have focused on the development of thought and institutions in early, especially second century, Christianity, and on the relationship of Luther to late medieval thought and piety. He was one of the original participants in the Lutheran-Catholic Dialogue, USA. Previous articles written for *Concilium* are 'Penance as a Separate Sacramental Sign' and 'Roman Primacy in the First Three Centuries'.

JOSEPH MOINGT, SJ, was born in 1915. A Jesuit, he taught theology at the Jesuit faculty at Fourvière (Lyon), then at the Institut Catholique de Paris. He is now teaching at the Institut supérieur de théologie et de philosophie de la Compagnie de Jésus in Paris (Sèvres Centre). Since 1969 he has been director of the review *Recherches de Science Religieuse* (Paris), and he has published numerous articles in other French religious and philosophical journals.

ALBERTO MOREIRA, OFM, was born in Anápolis-GO, Brazil, in 1955. He was ordained a priest in the Franciscan order in 1980. He studied at the Franciscan Theological Philosophical Institute in Petrópolis, Rio de Janeiro. For two years he worked with agricultural workers in the Pastoral Commission, CPT. He is currently a doctoral candidate in fundamental theology at the University of Münster.

ALPHONSE NGINDU MUSHETE was born in Tshilundu, Zaire, in 1937. He studied at the minor seminary of Kabwe, then in the major seminary in Mayidi before going on to the universities of Levanium, Louvain and Paris-Sorbonne. He took a first degree in social sciences before gaining a doctorate in theology in 1973 with a thesis on the problem of religious knowledge in the thought of L. Laberthonière. He is now professor of fundamental theology in the Catholic Faculty of Theology in Kinshasha. He was one of the founder members of the Ecumenical Association of Third World Theologians and has since 1979 edited the journal of the Ecumenical Association of African Theologians, the *Bulletin de Théologie Africaine*. Apart from his doctoral thesis, he has published various articles on theology in general and African theology in particular in *Revue du Clergé Africain, Revue d'Histoire Ecclesiastique, Le Monde Moderne* and *Problemi e prospettive di teologia dogmatica*.

ANDRÉ PAUL, Docteur en Théologie (Paris) and Docteur ès Lettres, also holds qualifications in Biblical Sciences (Rome) and Hebrew, Aramaic, Syriac and Ethiopian (Paris). He is a member of the Novi Testamenti Studiorum Societas and the European Association for Jewish Studies. He has many published works, his most recent books being *Le Monde juif à l'heure de Jésus* (1981) and *L'Inspiration et le canon des Ecritures* (1984).

TIEMO RAINER PETERS, OP, is a Dominican who was born in Hamburg and who studied philosophy and theology at Walberberg (Bonn) and Münster. He is a doctor of theology and is a member (*akademischer Rat*) of the Catholic faculty of theology at Münster university. His publications include: *Die Präsenz des Politischen in der Theologie D. Bonhoeffers* (1976); *Tod wird nicht mehr sein* (1978); (editor of) *Theologisch-politische Protokolle* (1981); *Steh auf und geh* (1984); *Een boodschap van vrede en vuur* (1986).

DOROTHEE SÖLLE was born in 1929. She studied theology, philosophy and literary criticism at Cologne, at Freiburg, and at Göttingen. She took her doctorate at Göttingen and her professorial exam at Cologne. She has been professor of systematic theology at Union Theological Seminary, New York, since 1975. Her publications include: *Stellvertretung, Ein Kapitel Theologie nach dem 'Tode Gottes'* (1965); *Atheistisch an Gott glauben* (1968); *Das Recht ein anderer zu werden* (1971); *Realisation. Studien zum Verhältnis von Theologie und Dichtung nach der Aufklärung* (1973); *Leiden-Themen der Theologie (1973); Die Hinreise. Zur religiösen Erfahrung* (1975); *Sympathie. Theologisch-politische Traktate* (1978); *Wählt das Leben* (1980); *Im Hause des Menschenfressers* (1981); *Aufrüstung tötet auch ohne Krieg* (1982); *Fürchte dich nicht, der Widerstand wächst* (1982); *Lieben und arbeiten. Eine Theologie der Schöpfung* (1985).

HERBERT VORGRIMLER was born in 1929 in Freiburg-im-Breisgau, West Germany. He studied philosophy and theology at the universities of Freiburg and Innsbruck, and since 1972 has been Professor of Dogmatics and the History of Dogma at the University of Münster in succession to his teacher, Karl Rahner. With Karl Rahner and others he produced the *Kleines theologisches Wörterbuch* (1985). His most recent book is *Theologische Gotteslehre* (1985)

ERICH ZENGER was born in 1939 in Dollnstein, Bavaria. He studied philosophy, theology and oriental languages in Rome, Jerusalem, Heidelberg and Münster. Since 1973 he has been professor for Old Testament exegesis in the Catholic theological faculty of Münster university. His publications include: *Die Sinaitheophanie* (1971); *Exodus. Geschichten und Geschichte der Befreiung Israels* (with P. Weimar) (2° 1982); *Durchkreuztes Leben. Hiob Hoffnung für die Leidenden* (3° 1982); *Das Buch Exodus* (2° 1982); *Der Gott der Bibel. Sachbuch zu den Anfängen des alttestamentlichen Gottesglaubens* (3° 1986); *Das Buch Judit* (1981); *Israel am Sinai. Analysen und Interpretationen zu Exodus 17–34* (2° 1985); *Gottes Bogen in den Wolken* (1983); *Das Buch Ruth* (1986).

CONCILIUM

CONCILIUM

CONCILIUM 1986

*All back issues are still in print: available from bookshops (price £4.95) or direct
from the publisher (£5.45/US$8.95/Can$10.95 including postage and packing).*

**T & T CLARK LTD, 59 GEORGE STREET
EDINBURGH EH2 2LQ, SCOTLAND**